LIVE TODAY WELL

Fr. Thomas F. Dailey, O.S.F.S.

LIVE TODAY WELL

ST. FRANCIS DE SALES'S SIMPLE APPROACH TO HOLINESS

SOPHIA INSTITUTE PRESS

Manchester, New Hampshire

Quotations from *Francis de Sales, Jane de Chantal: Letters of Spiritual Direction*, "Classics of Western Spirituality" series, translated by Péronne Marie Thibert, V.H.M., selected and introduced by Wendy M. Wright and Joseph F. Power, O.S.F.S., copyright © 1988 by Péronne Marie Thibert, V.H.M., Wendy M. Wright, and Joseph F. Power, O.S.F.S. New York/Mahwah, NJ: Paulist Press, 1988. Used with permission.

Quotations from Joseph Tissot, *How to Profit from Your Faults: Based on the Writings of St. Francis de Sales*, copyright © 2004 by Joseph Tissot, New York: Scepter Publishers, 2004. Used with permission.

Quotations from Francis de Sales, *Introduction to the Devout Life*, translated by John K. Ryan, copyright © 1950, 1952, 1966 by John K. Ryan, New York: Image Books, 1972/2003. Used with permission of Random House LLC.

Imprimi potest: Very Reverend James Greenfield, O.S.F.S., Provincial Superior

Nihil obstat: Reverend Monsignor James J. Mulligan, S.T.L.,
Censor Librorum, Diocese of Allentown

Imprimatur: Most Reverend John O. Barres, D.D., Bishop of Allentown

March 16, 2015

The *Nihil obstat* and *Imprimatur* are a declaration that a book or pamphlet is considered to be free from doctrinal or moral error. It is not implied that those who have granted the *Nihil obstat* and *Imprimatur* agree with the contents, opinions or statements expressed.

Sophia Institute Press
Box 5284, Manchester, NH 03108
1-800-888-9344

www.SophiaInstitute.com

Sophia Institute Press® is a registered trademark of Sophia Institute.

Library of Congress Cataloging-in-Publication Data
Dailey, Thomas F.
    Live today well : St. Francis de Sales's simple approach to holiness / Thomas F. Dailey, O.S.F.S.
        pages cm
    Includes bibliographical references.
    ISBN 978-1-62282-301-7 (pbk. : alk. paper) 1. Spiritual life—Catholic Church. 2. Francis, de Sales, Saint, 1567-1622. 3. Holiness—Catholic Church. I. Title.
    BX2350.3.D345 2015
    248.4'82—dc23
                                                                    2015013830

First printing

Let us be firmly resolved to serve God with our whole heart and life. Beyond that, let us have no care about tomorrow. Let us think only of *living today well*, and when tomorrow comes, it also will be today and we can think of it then.

—St. Francis de Sales, letter CXC,
to Mademoiselle de Soulfour, July 22, 1603

CONTENTS

ACKNOWLEDGMENTS

This guide to a good life comes from long ago and far away.

It originates with St. Francis de Sales (1567-1622), bishop of Geneva and Doctor of the Church. Recognized for his sanctity in his own lifetime, and revered by those who knew him as the "gentleman saint," Francis de Sales has bequeathed a corpus of writings that shape what is now called Salesian spirituality. Differing from the spiritual legacies of the great monastic schools (Augustinian, Benedictine, et cetera), the Salesian tradition exhibits a particular focus on living a life of holiness in the midst of the world.

Today Salesian spirituality serves as the cornerstone not only of religious orders and congregations but also of a growing number of lay movements in the Church. Its principles have been shaped into an educational philosophy at work in a number of apostolates affiliated with those groups. One such apostolate —DeSales University—gave rise to this guide.

In my dual roles there—as a faculty member in theology and as founding director of the Salesian Center for Faith and Culture—I have enjoyed the beauty of teaching Salesian spirituality, directly or indirectly, to traditional undergraduate students, to university employees, and to community members engaged in the center's programs and activities. From that experience I have rediscovered the appeal that this tradition holds and the power that it exercises on those who embrace it. That appeal, that power, that wisdom all come originally from the writings of St. Francis de Sales.

His classic devotional work, *Introduction to the Devout Life*, is the one with which St. Francis de Sales is most often and most readily identified. Even today's college students will read it! Some of them also study it, as do those who enroll in my course about the *Devout Life* as a great work of literature. It is from those students that I have learned. It is for those students — and others — that I write. And it is to all my students at DeSales University — past, present, and future — that I gratefully dedicate this work.

The writing of this book has benefited from the generosity of many persons, some of whom I mention here:

- The religious congregation of the Oblates of St. Francis de Sales (O.S.F.S.): My provincial superior, the Very Reverend James Greenfield, and my confreres in the Wills Hall Oblate Community, graciously accepted and made provision for the sabbatical leave during which the writing of this book took place. Their religious witness to Salesian spirituality is the lived experience on which this guide is based.

- The faculty, staff, administration, and trustees of DeSales University: DeSales University afforded me the opportunity to work on this project by granting a sabbatical leave from my faculty position during the 2013-2014 academic year. A particular debt of gratitude goes to Fr. John Fisher, O.S.F.S., and Lore McFadden-Westwood, who generously fulfilled my multiple responsibilities in the Salesian Center for Faith and Culture during my absence. The university's environment and the center's work form the context out of which this book grew and provide the arena in which I hope it will flourish.

- The faculty, students, staff, and administration of Saint Charles Borromeo Seminary, Overbrook, Pennsylvania: The historic seminary in the Archdiocese of Philadelphia provided a peaceful locale in which to write, and the people there graciously offered a fraternal spirit and prayerful community in which to live. By appointing me the inaugural John Cardinal Foley Chair in Homiletics and Social Communications at the seminary for the 2013-2014 academic year, Archbishop Charles Chaput allowed me to fashion a position that would carry on the work of St. Francis de Sales in the context of today's social communications.

My hope and my prayer is that this book will help to spread the Salesian charism, further the educational missions of DeSales University and Saint Charles Borromeo Seminary, and contribute to the Church's continuing work of evangelization. To one and all I express my deep gratitude.

LIVE TODAY WELL

INTRODUCTION

Long after his election, Pope Francis continues to garner the world's attention. His simple approach to holiness shows people how to see God in all things. His captivating words speak straight to the heart of all who hear or read them. His joyful exhortation to be near one another comes alive in so many hugs and smiles.

Four centuries ago, another Francis had a similar, although smaller, impact on the world of his day. One might even say that Francis de Sales—bishop, saint, and Doctor of the Church—was a precursor to today's more famous Francis.

Both share a name linked to Francis of Assisi. The pope explained his choice of a unique papal name as a remembrance of the patron saint of Italy, a man of peace and an advocate for the poor.[1] The saint, born prematurely in a room with an image of Francis of Assisi preaching to the birds and fish and other animals, would choose the Poverello as his personal patron saint.[2]

---

[1] The Holy Father explained the rationale for choosing the name Francis—the first time a pope has ever chosen this name—in a speech to representatives of the media three days after his election.

[2] Maurice Henry-Coüannier, *St. Francis de Sales and His Friends*, trans. Veronica Morrow (Staten Island, NY: Alba House, 1973), pp. 19-20.

As leaders, both were formed in the faith through years of Jesuit education. The pope's seminary training in the Society of Jesus shaped the habits and convictions with which he now guides the Church.[3] The saint, too, appropriated the Jesuit habit of mind through his studies in the Clermont College and at the Universities of Paris and Padua.[4]

As communicators, both convey a message of hope in simple yet imaginative ways that strike a popular chord in their listeners and readers. The pope has adopted new forms of teaching (e.g., interviews with journalists and meditations at daily Mass) in which he uses bold expressions that resonate with contemporary experience. The saint is admired for his personal correspondence and a voluminous body of writing that Elisabeth Stopp describes as revealing an "inspired common sense" in his guidance of souls.[5] In fact, the image of the Church as a "field hospital" that Pope Francis made famous in his first published interview is an image that Francis de Sales used in a sermon in 1619.[6]

---

[3] See Chris Lowney, *Pope Francis — Why He Leads the Way He Leads: Lessons from the First Jesuit Pope* (Chicago: Loyola Press, 2013).

[4] See Elisabeth Stopp, "Francis de Sales at Clermont College: A Jesuit Education in Sixteenth-Century Paris," in *A Man to Heal Differences: Essays and Talks on St. Francis de Sales* (Philadelphia: St. Joseph's University Press, 1997), pp. 23-50.

[5] Elisabeth Stopp, *St. Francis de Sales: Selected Letters* (New York: Harper and Row, 1960), pp. 33-34.

[6] Cf. Antonio Spadaro, S.J., "A Big Heart Open to God" (the exclusive interview with Pope Francis), *America*, September 30, 2013; Francis de Sales, Sermon for the Feast of SS. Cosmas and Damian, September 27, 1619, in *Oeuvres* IX:217.

As preachers, both express deep concern for homiletics as a pivotal means of proclaiming the gospel. Noting the quasi-sacramental character of what should be a brief but heart-to-heart communication,[7] the pope has repeatedly identified the homily as a touchstone of evangelization today. Similarly, the saint counseled other preachers about the necessity of speaking purposefully, pointedly, and cordially; he reminds us, even today, that the preacher's words "must issue from our heart rather than from our mouth" because "heart speaks to heart, and the tongue speaks only to men's ears."[8]

More than historical or literary coincidences, the traits shared by these churchmen flow from a mission common to both pope and saint: to proclaim the gospel in a manner that teaches, persuades, and motivates people to believe.

Fifty years after the Second Vatican Council, Pope Francis reminds us of the divine-human encounter that is the foundation of our human fulfillment:

 Thanks solely to this encounter — or renewed encounter — with God's love, which blossoms into an enriching friendship, we are liberated from our narrowness and self-absorption. We become fully human when we become more than human, when we let God bring us beyond

---

[7] Pope Francis, apostolic exhortation *Evangelii gaudium* ("The Joy of the Gospel"), November 24, 2013, nos. 135-159. See also Pope Francis's dialogue with seminarians in Rome, May 12, 2014.

[8] Francis de Sales, *On the Preacher and Preaching* (Chicago: Henry Regnery Co., 1964), 64. See also Jean Pierre Camus, *The Spirit of St. Francis de Sales, Bishop and Prince of Geneva* (London: Longmans, Green, 1921), pp. 279-299.

ourselves in order to attain the fullest truth of
our being. (*Evangelii gaudium*, no. 8)

So, too, for Francis de Sales, who lived and worked during the
Catholic Reformation following the Council of Trent: in his
spiritual masterpiece, *Introduction to the Devout Life*, he speaks
of being fully human in terms of "devotion" as it relates to our
vocation or state in life, for "wherever we may be, we can and
should aspire to a perfect life."[9]

The perfecting of human life in and through our relation to
God—this is the core of the teaching of both Francises. Put
simply, the pope and the saint both exhort us to *live today well*.

How to live today well is the subject of this book. The chapters
that follow bring the wisdom of St. Francis de Sales to light as a
sure means for dealing with, and thriving amid, the daily realities
of life in today's world.

The first part introduces the reader to some fundamental
tenets of Salesian spirituality. Personally experienced by the
saint and officially championed by Church leaders ever since,
"the devout life" appeals to people across the centuries precisely
because it is an *everyday* approach to holiness that enables us to
"be who we are and be that well."

[9] Francis de Sales, *Introduction to the Devout Life*, trans. and ed.
John K. Ryan (New York: Image Books, 2003), part 1, chap. 3, p.
33. (Hereafter, quotations from the *Introduction* will be cited in
text and referenced in terms of part, chapter, and page numbers
of this translation.)

INTRODUCTION

"[The Salesian] School created, by means of awakening the conscience to the truth of things, a Catholic culture that was not at all 'bigoted' or 'disoriented.' Study, the social values of living together, the social references to the neediest (I remember having learned there to deprive myself of some things to give to persons who were poorer than me), sport, competence, piety ... everything was real, and everything formed habits that, all together, molded a cultural way of being. One lived in this world but open to the transcendence of the other world. It was very easy for me later in secondary school, to make the 'transfer' (in the psycho-pedagogic sense) to other realities. And this simply because *I lived well* the realities lived in the School: without distortions, with realism, with a sense of responsibility and a horizon of transcendence."

—Father Jorge Mario Bergoglio (Pope Francis),
in a recollection about his education,
October 20, 1990 (emphasis added)

This approach to living well is encapsulated in a short text written by St. Francis de Sales called the *Spiritual Directory*, which is the primary subject of the second part of this book. Originally composed for a new religious order of nuns that he founded—the Visitation of Holy Mary—the saint's guidebook is modified and adapted here to the common dimensions of our daily routine. Through this adaptation the reader will experience the genius of the saint's pedagogy, which links our spiritual well-being to the ordinary events and present moments of everyday life.

Living each day well also entails other sacred moments, those that we choose to make part of our schedule on a daily basis or at regular intervals (weekly, monthly, or yearly). Part 3 considers a few such religious exercises, about which St. Francis de Sales reveals an uncanny understanding and for which he offers practical advice.

Throughout the book, readers will also find sidebars that offer additional information, drawn from the saint's other writings, about themes related to each chapter. And, for those who wish to delve more deeply into the richness of the Salesian tradition, a listing of helpful resources on how live well is provided in appendix 2.

From a sacred moment in the life of the Church that took place fifty years ago—the Second Vatican Council—we have inherited the call to be witnesses of holiness to the world. In continuity with that tradition, Pope Francis exhorts us to be "missionary disciples" in a Church that is "convinced, enthusiastic, certain and in love" with God, who walks with us, speaks to us, breathes in us, and works among us (*Evangelii gaudium*, no. 266).

St. Francis de Sales offers us a way to be and do just that. Of him, Paul VI wrote:

> No one of the recent Doctors of the Church more than St. Francis de Sales anticipated the deliberations and decisions of the Second Vatican Council with such a keen and progressive insight. He renders his contribution by the example of his life, by the wealth of his true and

sound doctrine, by the fact that he has opened and strengthened the spiritual ways of Christian perfection for all states and conditions in life. We propose that these three things be imitated, embraced, and followed.[10]

It may be ambitious, but the goal of this book is to help fulfill that threefold proposition.

---

[10] Pope Paul VI, *Sabaudiae gemma*, apostolic letter on the fourth centenary of the birth of St. Francis de Sales, January 29, 1967.

PART 1

SALESIAN SPIRITUALITY

This guide builds on the four-hundred-year-old tradition that bears the name Salesian spirituality. That tradition emerges from the life and writings of St. Francis de Sales, but it also benefits in essential ways from the lived insights of his closest friend and collaborator, St. Jane de Chantal (1572-1641). That tradition is embodied in the religious order of the Visitation of Holy Mary that together they founded. And that tradition continues to flourish not only among the Visitation Sisters but also among a growing number of religious congregations and lay societies that claim St. Francis de Sales as their patron.[11]

---

[11] Among which are those founded by St. John Bosco—the Salesians of Don Bosco (S.D.B.), the Daughters of Mary Help of Christians, and the Salesian Cooperators; those founded by Blessed Louis Brisson—the Oblate Sisters and the Oblates of St. Francis de Sales (O.S.F.S.); the Missionaries of St. Francis de Sales (M.S.F.S.) founded by Pierre-Marie Mermier; the lay Association of St. Francis de Sales; and the lay society of the Daughters of St. Francis de Sales.

1

THE DEVOUT LIFE

The seminal insight of the Salesian tradition remains as relevant today as it was in the saint's time — namely, that a life of devotion is a universal human calling, that holiness is possible in all walks of life, that a meaningful and fulfilling existence awaits all those who live well. Who better to guide us to that human destiny than one who knows the way from his own experience? As Pope Emeritus Benedict XVI said of him: "St. Francis de Sales is an exemplary witness of Christian humanism; with his familiar style, with words which at times have a poetic touch, he reminds us that human beings have planted in their innermost depths the longing for God and that in him alone can they find true joy and the most complete fulfillment."[12]

That witness begins with the saint's life, a story not easily condensed but a tale certainly worth telling. Others have written more detailed biographies.[13] Here we wish only to highlight a few

---

[12] Benedict XVI, general audience, March 2, 2011.

[13] For the best among English-language biographies, see Andre Ravier, S.J., *Francis de Sales: Sage and Saint* (San Francisco: Ignatius Press, 1988) and Joseph Boenzi, S.D.B., *Saint Francis de Sales: Life and Spirit* (Stella Niagra, NY: DeSales Resource, 2013).

aspects of his holy life that will shed some light on his distinct approach to spiritual well-being.

FRANCIS DE SALES: A VERY BRIEF BIOGRAPHY

Born in 1567, the first of thirteen children in an aristocratic family of Savoy (the region bounded today by parts of southern Switzerland, southeastern France, and northern Italy), Francis de Sales[14] was educated in the finer institutions of his time and place. At the College d'Annecy, he studied the French language, which he would learn and use so well that to this day his writings are studied in university courses on French literature. In Paris he undertook a thoroughly liberal arts curriculum, which also entailed lessons in nobility, such as horsemanship, fencing, and dancing. Add to this education a flavorful dose of Jesuit spirituality, and Francis would become the embodiment of the proverbial Renaissance man: astute, well-rounded, and virtuous. At the University of Padua he learned the finer points of jurisprudence, earning a dual doctorate in civil law and canon law at about the age of twenty-five. And in both university cities he also undertook, on his own initiative, the study of theology.

Two episodes from his university years would prove to be especially formative in the saint's life and later would become foundational to the spiritual guidance he offered to others.

[14] Francis was born to Francis de Boisy and Françoise de Sionnaz. Sales was the title of the estate where his father and uncle both lived. The name "de Sales" was given to all the children "at least until the day when Monsieur de Boisy would give them one of his estates." See Ravier, *Francis de Sales*, pp. 15-16.

The first happened in 1586 in Paris. During his studies there, he suffered an intense and sustained personal crisis — what today we might call clinical depression — during which he feared that he would be eternally damned. No one can determine for sure what actually caused such a traumatic experience in young Francis's life. It might have been physical fatigue, the energy of his many youthful endeavors finally wearing him out. It might have been intellectual consternation, the theological debates just not sitting well with him. It might have been a psychological complex, his naturally high anxiety yielding its destructive force on his delicate conscience.

Whatever the cause, this crisis would lead Francis to a spiritual conversion. After offering a prayer of abandonment to God's will before a statue of *Notre Dame de Bonne Délivrance* and reciting the well-known Memorare, he was mysteriously relieved of his troubles. From then on, he no longer sought holiness in the naïveté of romantic fervor; instead, he realized that whatever good he could muster and whatever bad he might suffer would be far and away surpassed by the mercy of God.[15] Appreciating the grace he received at that time, he committed himself to pray the Rosary every day.

The second spiritual turning point occurred in Padua. At this point in his intellectual formation, as a young man about to embark on the future, he realized that the environment in which he was living held many risks for the way of life he sought to lead. Padua was then a thriving university city, filled with the young

[15] For insights about this transformative event in the young saint's life, see the monograph entitled "Our Lady of Deliverance" published in 2004 by the Salesian Center for Faith and Culture at DeSales University.

and the restless — nearly twenty thousand students — amid a culture more secular than sacred. To aid his own maturity in the spiritual life there, he drew up for himself a personal rule of behavior, a series of five "spiritual exercises"[16] that he would later expand on and incorporate into his spiritual writings.

This habitual practice in Padua taught him that the natural affairs of human life are not to be set aside in the pursuit of supernatural growth and development. Rather, he came to understand that a devout life can be lived in and through our normal routines and responsibilities. But even there, or especially so, it became clear to him that "Christian life required strategy. A Christian should live *in* the world without being *of* the world, and to do this required art."[17] Later the saint would teach this art to his spiritual children with exercises that would enable them to live devoutly, even today.

After returning to his native Savoy, Francis de Sales entered upon his ecclesial vocation. He was named provost of the cathedral chapter of Geneva, a quasi-political position that put him second in rank to the local bishop. That assignment satisfied, to some degree, his father's aspirations that his eldest son would become a diplomat. But Francis had another career path in mind!

He was ordained to the priesthood at the age of twenty-six. Soon thereafter he volunteered for a "missionary" assignment to the Chablais (the area surrounding the southern side of Lake Geneva). At the time, the formerly Catholic region had become thoroughly Calvinist, so much so that local policy prohibited public interaction with the papist preacher.

---

[16] St. Francis de Sales, *Spiritual Exercises*, trans. William N. Dougherty, ed. Joseph Chorpenning (Toronto: Peregrina, 1993).
[17] E. J. Lajeunie, quoted in *Spiritual Exercises*, p. 10.

Yet preach he did! He also conducted public liturgical celebrations and held private theological conversations with Protestant leaders. There, too, he devised an ingenious means of teaching about Catholicism through printed pamphlets, a novel technique for which he would later be named the patron saint of Catholic journalists and writers.[18]

His experience in that missionary adventure gave rise to a key dimension of the Salesian approach to holiness. Known today as "the Chablais spirit,"[19] this approach emphasizes not a fire-and-brimstone brand of apologetics, nor a military-style discipline in terms of spirituality. Rather, Francis de Sales adopted a dialogic approach, one that pursues the lofty and grace-filled heights of holiness by way of the very real and concrete situations in which people find themselves. His method was to inspire and persuade rather than to demand and compel. He lived by a motto he would later counsel other religious authorities to follow—namely, to do all through love and nothing by force.[20]

By all accounts, his method worked exceptionally well in the Chablais, as he was credited with reconverting some seventy-two thousand people! (And as history has shown, it still works ... in those whom we celebrate as saints in their own right and in

---

[18] These writings would be collected in a work mistakenly titled *The Catholic Controversy*. On this and related stories about his evangelizing work, see the collection of articles by Herbert Winklehner on "St. Francis de Sales: Patron of Journalists," published as a monograph in 2004 by the Salesian Center for Faith and Culture at DeSales University.

[19] Cf. J. Chorpenning, "What Is the 'Chablais Spirit'?" in the *ICSS Newsletter*, no. 18, July 2006.

[20] Letter to Jane de Chantal, October 14, 1604, in *Letters of Spiritual Direction*, p. 134.

ST. JANE DE CHANTAL (1572–1641)

Jane Frances Fremyot was born of a prominent family in Dijon, France. At the age of twenty, she married Christopher de Rabutin, Baron de Chantal. They had six children (of whom four survived into adulthood) and enjoyed a happy marriage. When her husband was killed by a family friend in a hunting accident in 1601, she became desolate and sought spiritual guidance in her grief.

In the wake of her husband's death, Jane and her children went to live with her father-in-law, a thoroughly unpleasant and difficult man who, among other things, kept a mistress. As if her grief and the task of raising young children alone were not enough of a burden, Jane de Chantal eventually found herself trying to manage the financial affairs of her father-in-law's estate. Through it all, her faith in God and her love for others deepened.

In 1604, she met Francis de Sales in her hometown of Dijon, France, where the young bishop was preaching a Lenten mission. He was deeply touched by her passion for God and the things of God. He became her spiritual director, and their friendship would grow and thrive throughout his lifetime.

Together with Bishop de Sales, Jane de Chantal began the religious Order of the Visitation of Holy Mary in Annecy with three other women: Jacqueline Favre, Charlotte de Bréchard, and Anne Coste. They were to be daughters of prayer who lived the life of the gentle, humble Jesus through the practice of the little virtues and the cultivation of a community life that balanced prayer and activity.

Even by today's standards, Jane de Chantal was a capable administrator in her own right, as evidenced by the fact that over eighty Visitation communities had been established by the time of her death at Moulins on December 13, 1641. She was canonized by Pope Clement XIII in 1767. Her remains are preserved, alongside those of St. Francis de Sales, in the Basilica of the Visitation in Annecy.

the innumerable lives of those who have embraced the Salesian tradition.)

Not long after his mission to the Chablais region, Francis de Sales was consecrated bishop of Geneva on December 8, 1602. With the teachings of the Council of Trent still being implemented at that time, he committed himself to educate the people of his diocese about the doctrines of the Church. He did so by preaching frequently, organizing diocesan synods, and initiating parish visitations. He was a gifted educator who created the Confraternity of Christian Doctrine (CCD) and personally directed catechism classes, once even managing to teach prayers to a young man unable to hear (which would lead to Francis's being named patron saint of the deaf). He established a liberal arts school—the Florimontane Academy[21]—whose original members would later be instrumental in founding today's revered French Academy.

---

[21] A summary of the story of this academy can be found on the website of the Salesian Center for Faith and Culture.

Throughout his episcopacy, the bishop was known for encountering people wherever they were, commoner and scholar alike, saints and sinners together. Besieged by administrative concerns that are commonplace today, such as financial troubles and personnel issues, and bewildered by a lack of religious discipline and practice just as evident today, Francis de Sales approached the spiritual life as something requiring continual development in the face of repeated failure. The key to growth in holiness, he would constantly teach, is always to begin again, to keep moving forward, confident that the good Lord will provide.

During his time as bishop of Geneva, two significant developments contributed to the establishment and flowering of what would later be called Salesian spirituality.

The first was the founding of the religious order of the Visitation of Holy Mary in 1610 together with Jane de Chantal, who would herself be canonized. Francis's relationship with Jane is a classic example of true spiritual friendship[22] and their lifelong collaboration the embodiment of a spiritual wisdom that grew through mutual development.

For Francis and Jane, the founding of the Visitation was to be a unique venture. Unlike other religious orders, this one was not originally established on the traditional vows of chastity, poverty, and obedience; instead, the Sisters were to "have no bond but the bond of love."[23] Moreover, this group of nuns did not undertake rigorous practices of mortification; instead, they

---

[22] See Wendy M. Wright, *Bond of Perfection: Jeanne de Chantal and François de Sales* (Paulist Press, 1986).

[23] Francis de Sales, "Spiritual Directory for the Religious Sisters of the Visitation of Holy Mary," *Oeuvres* XXV:135.

would practice what St. Jane describes as a "martyrdom of love" toward each other,[24] which focused on daily acts of charity and included an occasional visit to town to care for people in need.

In time, the Visitation would forego doing apostolic works outside the monastery and submit to a cloistered way of life under a traditional monastic rule. This canonical change demonstrated the saints' shared understanding that holiness was focused not on specific activities but on the humble and gentle spirit with which these women were to cultivate the spiritual life in obedience to God's will. To do all and accept all in concert with God is the foundational principle of Salesian spirituality. The *Spiritual Directory* that St. Francis de Sales wrote for these Sisters puts this principle into action as a daily guide to a good life. To this day, the nuns in Visitation monasteries around the world practice that simple life, without pious austerities, yet with great fervor in their shared quest for holiness.

The second significant facet of Francis's time as bishop was his work as a spiritual director. Despite the burdens of his office, he spent time each day writing to those who sought his aid; it is estimated that he penned more than ten thousand letters of spiritual direction[25] — in an age long before e-mail and text messaging! Based on these letters and on his continual reflection on human life as graced by God, he wrote two books that have become spiritual classics: *Introduction to the Devout Life* (1610

---

[24] See Françoise-Madeleine de Changy, ed., *Memoirs sur la vie et les vertus de Saint J.-F. de Chantal* (Paris 1853), vol. 3, pp. 306-307.

[25] Cf. *St. Francis de Sales: Selected Letters*; *Francis de Sales, Jane de Chantal: Letters of Spiritual Direction*; and *Thy Will Be Done: Letters to Persons in the World* (Manchester, NH: Sophia Institute Press, 1995).

and never out of print since then) and a *Treatise on the Love of God* (1616).[26]

His exhausting work came to an end in 1622, when he died at the Visitation monastery in Lyons, after traveling on a diplomatic mission to Avignon and making a final visit with St. Jane de Chantal. He was canonized by Pope Alexander VII in 1661 and was declared a Doctor of the Church by Pope Pius IX in 1878.

That latter designation attests to the spiritual genius of St. Francis de Sales's many writings. There one will find instructions, exhortations, consolations and a host of explanations on how to live well amid the myriad challenges of life and love, of virtue and sin, of sickness and death that people face every day and about which people sought St. Francis's advice in his day.

Introduction to the Devout Life, in particular, encapsulates the genius of Salesian spirituality and makes it applicable in every age and place. It teaches the reader how to "be who you are and be that well." This exhortation, taken from one of the saint's letters, serves as a tagline for the Salesian approach to the good life. In its original context, it unites three key dimensions to living well: a humble recognition of the rootedness of our human existence and the gentle pursuit of that which we can and should be as persons, all within the parameters of divine providence. Here is the full quotation:

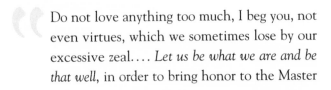

> Do not love anything too much, I beg you, not even virtues, which we sometimes lose by our excessive zeal.... *Let us be what we are and be that well*, in order to bring honor to the Master

---

[26] Various editions of both works are listed in appendix 2. Citations in this book come from the translation by Dom B. Mackey.

Craftsman whose handiwork we are. People laughed at the painter who, intending to paint a horse, came up with a perfect bull; the work was handsome in itself, but not much credit to the artist who had had other plans and succeeded in this one only by chance. *Let us be what God wants us to be*, provided we are His, and let us not be what we would like to be, contrary to His intention. Even if we were the most perfect creatures under heaven, what good would that do us if we were not as God's will would have us be? (*Letters of Spiritual Direction*, p. 111, emphasis added)

For St. Francis de Sales, becoming what God has created us to be is the goal of human life and the singular way to find real happiness. He calls this the devout life. Others would call it holiness. We might call it simply the good life—the life we are all called to live well by the God who gave life to each of us.

In his particular understanding of what that life entails, the saint makes two important distinctions, which he explains at the outset of his *Introduction to the Devout Life*. First, he posits a difference between false and true devotion. A common view of holiness links it to identifiably religious deeds, such as disciplinary acts by an individual (e.g., fasting) or charitable acts for others (e.g., service) or spiritual acts toward God (e.g., prayers). For Francis de Sales, however, true devotion—like true love—is first and foremost a matter of the human heart.

Emanating from that personal center, devotion brings together the interior dimension (our heart) and the exterior dimension (our actions) to make life well-integrated, to make us whole. As he further explains it:

> Genuine, living devotion ... presupposes love of God, and hence it is simply true love of God. Yet it is not always love as such. Inasmuch as divine love adorns the soul, it is called grace, which makes us pleasing to his Divine Majesty. Inasmuch as it strengthens us to do good, it is called charity. When it has reached a degree of perfection at which it not only makes us do good but also do this carefully, frequently, and promptly, it is called devotion. (*Introduction*, part 1, chap. 1, p. 28)

Put simply: living today well means fulfilling life's responsibilities, no matter what they are, in a way that strives for good in response to God's grace. We live this good life *carefully* when we do what we do with intentionality, rather than by accident or out of mere routine. We live this good life *frequently* when we do so by taking advantage of the opportunities given to us each day rather than only occasionally. We live this good life *promptly* when we act not in a calculated way — as in "what can I get out of this?" — but by being immediately responsive to the needs of others. As the saint says, "In short, devotion is simply that spiritual agility and vivacity by which [divine] charity works in us or by aid of which we work quickly and lovingly" (*Introduction*, part 1, chap. 1, 28-29).

A second clarification concerns the very possibility of living this kind of life. Presaging what the Second Vatican Council taught as "the universal call to holiness in the Church,"[27] Francis

---

[27] See chapter 5 of *Lumen gentium*, the dogmatic constitution on the Church, November 21, 1964.

de Sales championed the notion that holiness is possible for all people, not just those with a religious calling or profession. He states forthrightly:

> It is an error, or rather a heresy, to wish to ban-ish the devout life from the regiment of soldiers, the mechanic's shop, the court of princes, or the home of married people. It is true ... that purely contemplative, monastic, and religious devotion cannot be exercised in such states of life. However, besides those three kinds of de-votion there are several others adapted to bring perfection to those living in the secular state.... Wherever we may be, we can and should aspire to a perfect life. (*Introduction*, part 1, chap. 3, pp. 32-33)

Here the Doctor of the Church makes a distinction between different kinds of devotion. As there are different vocations or states in life to which we are called, so there are differences in what holiness means for each of us. This distinction has two important implications.

On the one hand, it renders the devout life very flexible. It recognizes that the practice of holiness must be adapted to dif-ferent occupations and situations, according to different times and places, and in fulfillment of different duties and responsibili-ties. On the other hand, the adaptability of the devout life does not mean that holiness is purely relative, that each person can decide what it means and how to live it. As previously stated, there are such things as *true* and *false* when it comes to devo-tion. For Francis de Sales, the real test of a good life is whether our devotion is in keeping with our state in life and whether it enriches who we are in that vocation.

Thus, to "be who you are and be that well" means to recognize and respond to the moments of grace and the opportunities for charity that are presented to us each and every day. To live these moments well, St. Francis de Sales offers us a guide—the *Spiritual Directory*—that takes into account the basic elements common to everyone's daily life.

2

ST. FRANCIS'S
SPIRITUAL DIRECTORY

Compared with other texts in the extensive *Oeuvres* of St. Francis de Sales, the *Spiritual Directory* is a tiny gem.[28] This booklet is neither a doctrinal exposition nor a spiritual treatise. It is a series of exercises that pertain to the customs of religious life. It thus serves as a spiritual guide for beginners who wish to live each day in union with God.

Intended for the private audience of the Visitation Sisters, the final text of the *Directory* was edited by St. Jane de Chantal. After the death of Francis de Sales, she set herself to the task of gathering all his writings. Then, with the assistance of the superiors of other Visitation monasteries in which various manuscripts were circulating, she proceeded to amend and correct the custom book. What they eventually produced, around 1635, was

---

[28] For an explication of the continuing transmission of this text, see T. Dailey, "Jewel of Perfection: The *Spiritual Directory* as a Privileged Means of Propagating the Salesian Spirit," in *Indian Journal of Spirituality* 21/4 (2008): 349-362.

the *Spiritual Directory* as the founding Father had intended it for his new religious order.[29]

Like similar "custom books" of the time, the *Spiritual Directory* guides the particular way of life in a monastery. As Fr. Alexander Pocetto explains, these books "had a twofold purpose: (1) to give the Rule and the Constitutions of a particular order or congregation its specific and distinguishing characteristic, and (2) to create a common spiritual life that would transcend cultures and countries." A directory accomplishes this dual purpose by specifying the obligations each nun is to perform out of love for God and by motivating her to do so. In this way, it serves as the raison d'être of the lived reality of the community.[30]

Then, as now, the *Spiritual Directory* has served as a code of sanctification for those inspired by Salesian spirituality.[31] Fr. Jean Gayet describes it as "nothing else than the ensemble of practical, concrete, daily means, practiced by St. Francis de Sales in

---

[29] The history of its formulation and the final version of the text are found in the *Oeuvres*, vol. 25, pp. 133-175. A translation of the complete text, as adapted for contemporary use by the Oblates of St. Francis de Sales, is given in appendix 1.

[30] A. Pocetto, "The *Spiritual Directory* in the American Oblate Tradition," Salesian Center for Faith and Culture.

[31] The *Spiritual Directory* continues to support the religious charism of the Visitation Sisters, as well as that of the Oblate Sisters and Oblates of St. Francis de Sales. It has also been adapted for other groups, such as P. Pernin, *Spiritual Guide for Priests: The Spiritual Directory of St. Francis de Sales* (New York: Paulist Press, 1918); F. Fox, *A Spiritual Directory for People in the World* (Baltimore: Carroll Press, 1950); J. Woods, *The Spiritual Directory of St. Francis de Sales for People Living in the World* (Westminster, MD: Newman Press, 1959); and L. Fiorelli, *Spiritual Directory of St. Francis de Sales: Reflections for the Laity* (Boston: Pauline Books, 1985).

order to sanctify himself and lead to perfection the souls whom he directed."[32] Sr. Marie-Esperance Charlier calls it "the daily route that Saint Francis de Sales proposes to us so that we might not lose sight of our intended goal [union with God] nor distance ourselves from the Savior's company."[33]

Adapted here for life in the twenty-first century, the *Spiritual Directory* makes visible the glamour of holiness for anyone desiring or seeking the good life. Its distinctive radiance creates an aura of sanctity in everyone who lives by it, because it enables people today to be claimed by the divine Spirit of love that is our human origin and end. Fidelity to its teaching leads the Salesian disciple to die to his own preferences and inclinations and to live continuously in the presence of God. Union with God is the ultimate goal of living well in every age. It fulfills the wish of the saintly founders for their religious order, as St. Jane de Chantal explains in the introduction to the *Spiritual Directory*:

 The intention of our holy Father [Francis de Sales] was that our whole life and all our works be dedicated to union with God, so that we might assist in the renewal of the Church and the salvation of our neighbor by our prayer, works and good example, and that we might excel in every kind of virtue — this he desired more than anything else.[34]

---

[32] J. Gayet, "Le Directoire spiritual de Saint François de Sales" (unpublished paper), pp. 1, 2.

[33] Cited in L. Fiorelli, "The Spiritual Directory Today" (unpublished paper), p. 5.

[34] St. Jane de Chantal composed this "intention" for the beginning of the custom book of 1624 and later added it to the version of the *Spiritual Directory* that was published in 1633.

That intention forms the structural basis of the *Spiritual Directory* as it was originally conceived. Likewise, it provides a solid base for the renewal of Christian life, individually and collectively, in the contemporary world.

On the one hand, the *Directory* builds on the essential link between who we are and what we do—that is, "our whole life and all our works." In this anthropological vision, actions exhibit the power to transform people, to shape and constitute our lives according to what we seek most. When that desire is "dedicated to union with God," our actions can make us into saints. In this way, Salesian spirituality sees in Christian living much more than social activism or personal piety; the Salesian ethic, instead, seeks the perfection of life and of love.

On the other hand, this personal transformation holds the key to the renewal of the Church as a whole. In a Salesian ecclesiology, the Church is not primarily a worship site or a sociological institution. It is, first and foremost, a communion of saints—those already so in heaven and those aspiring to be so. When her members lead the good life, when they "excel in every kind of virtue," the Church becomes what she is and fulfills her mission of bringing the Good News of salvation to the world.

SALESIAN PEDAGOGY

St. Francis de Sales is recognized as a Doctor of the Church due to his uncanny ability to communicate the truths of Christian belief and to inspire the holiness of Christian life. He does this, according to Oblate Father Roger Balducelli, by adopting a well-calculated pedagogical strategy in his formulation of the *Spiritual Directory*:

> Since Salesian spirituality is nothing but a quest for the love of God, the *Directory* enjoys within the economy of that spirituality a privileged status. It brings it to fruition. From the level of conception and speech, it moves the spiritual doctrine to the level of existence by making that which the spiritual discourse is about a modification of that which the discourse is for, namely, a modification of consciousness and life.[35]

That twofold modification happens in concert with, and as a result of, the distinct method for directing souls to God that St. Francis de Sales championed. Three principles characterize this Salesian approach to the good life.

First, the saint situates the pursuit of holiness within the *everyday experience* of our lives, in two senses of that term. On the one hand, he considers the pursuit of holiness as a phenomenon contained in or contextualized by the period of each and every day. In his view, the present moment of today is the only one at our disposal and thus is the only time over which we have any direct control. By focusing our energies there, we are more likely to remain at peace, neither disturbed about the past nor anxious about the future. Thus, his advice to one of his spiritual daughters (Mademoiselle de Soulfour) serves as a summary statement of the spiritual life—just as it also provides the overarching theme of this book:

[35] Roger Balducelli, O.S.F.S., "A Commentary on the Spiritual Directory of the Oblates of St. Francis de Sales" (unpublished manuscript, 1973), chap. 2, pp. 2-3.

> Let us be firmly resolved to serve God with our
> whole heart and life. Beyond that, let us have
> no care about tomorrow. Let us think only of
> *living today well*, and when tomorrow comes it
> also will be today and we can think about it
> then. (*Letters of Spiritual Direction*, pp. 98-99,
> emphasis added)

On the other hand, St. Francis de Sales considers the ordinary, everyday experience of life as providing the best opportunities for living well. For him, spirituality is not one of the multiple aspects of our lives; rather, it offers a comprehensive approach to the whole of life and is put into practice through the normal activities and regular responsibilities we carry out each day. From that perspective, he sees holiness not as the practice of heroic feats of sanctity, but as doing what we naturally do with a supernatural impetus. He explains it this way:

> Occasions do not often present themselves for
> the exercise of fortitude, magnanimity, and
> great generosity, but meekness, temperance,
> integrity, and humility are virtues that must
> mark all our actions in life.... In practicing
> the virtues, we should prefer the one most
> conformable to our duties rather than the one
> more agreeable to our tastes. (*Introduction*, part
> 3, chap. 1, p. 111)

With its focus on the everydayness of the spiritual life, the second principle of Salesian pedagogy acknowledges that personal growth takes place "little by little." The saint's grasp of human nature is such that he knows we do not change our lives all at once. He recognizes, from his own experience, that personal transformation is a lifelong process and that it does not come easy. For that reason, he often reminds people not to be overwhelmed by their desire for holiness but instead to attend to their spiritual growth gently, by taking small yet continual steps forward. As he writes in one of his letters:

> I don't mean that we shouldn't head in the direction of perfection, but that we mustn't try to get there in a day, that is, a mortal day, for such a desire would upset us, and for no purpose. In order to journey steadily, we must apply ourselves to doing well the stretch of road immediately before us on the first day of the journey, and not waste time wanting to do the last lap of the way while we still have to make it through the first. (*Letters of Spiritual Direction*, p. 97)

Along this spiritual journey, the third principle of Salesian pedagogy recognizes that personal transformation works most effectively when it moves from "inside out." In keeping with his profound respect for human freedom,[36] Francis de Sales is convinced that persuasion always works better than compulsion:

---

[36] Cf. his *Treatise on the Love of God*, trans. Dom B. Mackey (Rockford, IL: TAN Books, 1997), book 2, chap. 12, p. 95: "we are not drawn to God by iron chains, as bulls and wild oxen, but by enticements, sweet attractions, and holy inspirations, which, in a word, are the *cords of Adam*, and of humanity, that is, proportionate and adapted to the human heart, to which liberty is

> I cannot approve the methods of those who try to reform a man by beginning with outward things, such as his bearing, dress, or hair. On the contrary, it seems to me that we ought to begin inside him.... Since the heart is the source of our actions, as the heart is, so are they.... In short, whoever wins a man's heart has won the whole man. Yet even the heart, where we wish to begin, must be instructed as to how it should model its outward conduct and bearing so that by them men can see not only holy devotion but also great wisdom and prudence. (*Introduction,* part 3, chap. 23, p. 172)

The goal of the *Spiritual Directory* is to provide that very instruction of the heart. This it does by suggesting various ways to keep one's heart in the presence of God throughout the day and by doing so to transform daily activities into means of sanctification, a lesson Francis de Sales first taught himself as a young student at the University of Padua.

Through a series of daily spiritual exercises, the saint seeks to lead us to the singular exercise of living well. He wishes to transform the natural human inclination to love into a personal mode of existing always in relation to God. Thus, our existential project entails learning how to live fully, in view of our mortality,

---

natural." (Hereafter, quotations from the *Treatise* will be cited in text and referenced by book, chapter, and page numbers of this translation.) See also Eunan McDonnell, *The Concept of Freedom in the Writings of St. Francis de Sales* (New York: Peter Lang, 2009).

and how to find meaning in a life that, without God, would otherwise succumb to futility. We learn this best, according to the saintly Doctor, not by hearing or reading but by doing; we progress toward this ultimate goal not by cognitional development but by existential experience. In this vein, the *Spiritual Directory* teaches us to act in such a way that we become, through practice, ever more conscious of the divine presence in our midst and ever more intentional in the human choices we make in response to that presence. These spiritual exercises make it possible to learn to love God. As Fr. Balducelli puts it, "by making an infinite use of finite means, the threshold of infinity itself has been reached."

To cross that threshold in this world is to "live Jesus,"[37] and St. Francis de Sales's pedagogical strategy intends to show people how to do this. Focusing on the ordinary dimensions of human life, St. Francis's pragmatic approach recognizes that we begin the spiritual quest anew each day, yet always from an advanced starting point, until one day we arrive at our eternal salvation. This strategy underlies the *Spiritual Directory* and offers a proven method for living well. That such a life will result in genuine happiness is the point Francis makes in the preface to this spiritual gem.

---

[37] As a young student, Francis de Sales would write the French initials "V+J" (for *Vive + Jesus*) at the top of his notebook pages as a reminder to "live Jesus" in all his deeds. Later, he concludes the *Treatise on the Love of God* with these words: "To love or to die! To die and to love! To die to all other love in order to live to Jesus' love, that we may not die eternally, but that, living in thy eternal love, O Saviour of our souls we may eternally sing: *Vive Jésus*! I love Jesus. Live Jesus whom I love! I love Jesus, who lives and reigns forever and ever. Amen" (XII:12, p. 555).

THE RULE OF PADUA

In his introduction to St. Francis de Sales's *Spiritual Exercises*, Oblate Father Joseph Chorpenning quotes St. Ignatius of Loyola to explain that "we call Spiritual Exercises every way of preparing and disposing the soul to rid itself of all inordinate attachments, and, after their renewal, of seeking and finding the will of God in the disposition of our life for the salvation of our soul" (p. 11). With that goal in mind, and having benefited from his own Jesuit education, a young Francis de Sales (age twenty-one to twenty-five) composed five such exercises for himself, which have come to be known as the Rule of Padua:

1. "Exercise of the Preparation of the Day," whose purpose was "to help [him] avoid offending God and to avail himself of opportunities to serve God that present themselves during the day" (p. 14)

2. "Rules for Spending the Day Well," by which he aimed "to structure [his] day through a program of prayer so that he effectively keeps his focus fixed on God from the moment of awakening in the morning to that of retiring at night" (p. 15)

3. "Exercise of Spiritual Sleep or Repose," in which he fostered a grateful recognition of divine blessings received so that he might, in turn, serve well the divine source of those gifts

4. "Rules for Conversation and Social Gatherings," through which he could integrate his quest for devotion

and his stately responsibilities in the social circles he
was obliged to frequent

5. "Frequent Communion," in which the future saint
   spells out how he will prepare and give thanks for
   the reception of the Blessed Sacrament

As Fr. Chorpenning notes, these exercises provide "a first-
hand glimpse of the Saint as a young man ... struggling to
respond to the divine invitation to union in an environment
hardly conducive to such a response" (p. 8). Today we face a
similar struggle to lead the good life, and the practical wisdom
sown in the young saint's exercises will later blossom in his
Introduction to the Devout Life and *Spiritual Directory* — as we
will explore in the chapters that follow.

THE PREFACE TO THE
SPIRITUAL DIRECTORY[38]

St. Francis de Sales opens his code of sanctification with a meditation on Sacred Scripture[39] that serves as an exhortation for a

---

[38] The preface to the *Spiritual Directory* includes this opening exhortation as well as three "wishes" of St. Francis de Sales for the new
religious order. These texts were not part of the original *Directory*
but were written by the saint as the preface to the Constitutions
for the Visitation Sisters (*Oeuvres* XXV:23-24).

[39] Ezekiel 2:8-3:3; cf. Revelation 10. On this biblical passage, see
Margaret S. Odell, "You Are What You Eat: Ezekiel and the

renewed experience of the sacred by those who will practice what he preaches in the *Spiritual Directory*:

> Come, O children blessed from all eternity, and as was said to Ezekiel and to St. John the Evangelist: Come, take hold of this book and eat it, swallow it, fill your heart and nourish your soul with it. Let its words remain day and night before your eyes that you may meditate on them and in your hands that you may put them into practice, and let your entire being praise God for them. This book will prove bitter to your interior, for it will lead to the perfect mortification of your self-love. It will, on the other hand, be sweeter than honey in your mouth because there is no consolation equal to that of mortifying our self-love in order to let live and reign in us the love of him who died for love of us. In this way your bitterness will be transformed into the sweetness of a perfect peace, and you will be filled with true happiness.
>
> I ask you, my children, nay rather I beg and exhort you, be strong, firm, persevering, unchanging and so remain in order that nothing

---

Scroll," *Journal of Biblical Literature* 117/2 (1998): 229-248. Also included in this preface are allusions to the book of Joshua (1:8—on reciting and observing the book of the law), to the Psalms (e.g., 103:1—"Bless the Lord, O my soul; and all that is within me, bless his holy name!"), to the Acts of the Apostles (4:32—on the community as one in heart and mind), and to the book of Revelation (22:6-7—on the blessed life).

may separate you from Jesus Christ who has
brought you together, nor from that community
which can keep you one with him, so that, all
of you having but one heart and one mind, he
himself may be your only mind and heart.

Blessed the person who lives by this Rule, for
it is reliable and true. May the grace, peace and
consolation of the Holy Spirit be given abundantly and forever to all who follow it. Amen.

Francis de Sales invites us with some urgency—*come*—to
experience the same sacred vision as did two great religious figures of old. With a bit of literary embellishment, he commends
the very same actions the Lord requires in the visions of Ezekiel
and John: *Take hold,* for the doing of these exercises requires an
intentional effort. *Eat* and *swallow,* for simply having this text in
one's possession is not enough. *Fill* and *nourish* those dimensions
to being human (heart and soul) that are in need of sustenance
and cannot be satisfied other than in God.

Francis first extends the invitation to our *eyes*—the doors to
the mind and the place of comprehension. But for this wise saint,
knowing does not suffice for living well. And so he exhorts us to
take up the challenge in our *hands,* for no matter what responsibility we have to fulfill or what task we have to perform, our
work can and should be sanctified. Ultimately, he extends this
experience of the sacred to our *entire being,* as persons created
in the image and likeness of God and destined for union with
God in eternity.

But that experience will not be easy! Contrary to the preferred tastes of our secular culture, contrary even to our own
preferences and inclinations, the path set forth in this little book

charts a course of life and love that will draw us out of ourselves and toward God, to whom we are naturally inclined. In reaffirming our willingness to serve God more so than ourselves, St. Francis acknowledges that this first taste of detachment may be bitter to swallow, but it cannot be avoided if we wish to become who we are to be. In a culture that claims widespread spiritual believing despite less religious belonging, the *Spiritual Directory* provides a worthwhile antidote to the individualism and relativism that falsely purport to fill our human longing for something more.

Once digested, the manner of living counseled in these pages will ultimately give a sweeter taste and a lasting consolation, through the filling of our hearts and souls with the crucified Jesus—"who died for love of us"—so that even today we may experience that divine love. This is what claims our deepest desire—an experience, like his, of a death that enables life. It is, ultimately, our experience of the sacred here and now. In a culture that longs for hope, the practice of the *Spiritual Directory* generates peace and tranquillity.

Living well in this way leads to genuine happiness. It is not difficult to imagine that a false happiness exists; our culture offers images of it in many ways, few of which connect happiness to what is religious. Fortunately, there is another story to be told. In a culture enamored of self-help processes and personages, the *Spiritual Directory* reaches even higher, leading its practitioners from the imminent to the transcendent, from the natural to the supernatural, from the secular to the sacred.

Through the saintly examples of those who have embodied it, we know that Salesian spirituality offers a sure way to experience the heavenly peace that the secular world cannot give. We see this in the Visitation order, through the lives of St. Jane de

Chantal, St. Margaret Mary Alacoque, and the blessed martyrs of Madrid. We find it in St. Vincent de Paul and St. John Bosco, who both placed themselves under the patronage of Francis de Sales, and in the saintly men and women associated with the religious congregations and lay associations they founded. More recently, we have witnesses to this in the founders of the Oblates of St. Francis de Sales: St. Léonie Aviat and Blessed Louis Brisson.

We, too, can actually be happy—when our lives and work are grounded in an experience of holiness, as the exercises of the *Spiritual Directory* will demonstrate. Thus, with St. Francis de Sales as our guide, we are invited anew to discover everything that can be sacred in our life. So, *come, O children*, and through the saintly advice offered here, embrace the "one heart and one mind" that unites us to God in Jesus Christ. Live today well, and the "grace, peace and consolation of the Holy Spirit" will be yours!

PART 2

OUR DAILY ROUTINE

The *Spiritual Directory* written by Francis de Sales and revised by Jane de Chantal contains a series of articles corresponding to different activities of each day. They arranged it this way to transform mundane matters into sacred moments. To accomplish this, the saints suggest making use of a variety of prayerful *aspirations* while carrying out each of our daily actions.

What are aspirations? In Salesian spirituality, they are biblical or other verbal expressions that convey short, ardent movements of the heart toward God. The purpose of these prayers is to remind us of God's loving presence, even in worldly matters, and to arouse affection for God in all things. In his *Introduction to the Devout Life*, St. Francis de Sales elaborates on this purpose with a charming comparison:

If our mind thus habituates itself to intimacy, privacy, and familiarity with God, it will be completely perfumed by his perfections. There is no difficulty in this exercise, as it may be

> interspersed among all our tasks and duties with-
> out any inconvenience, since in this spiritual
> retirement or amid these interior aspirations
> we only relax quickly and briefly. This does not
> hinder but rather assists us greatly in what we
> do. The pilgrim who takes a little wine to restore
> his heart and refresh his mouth stops for a while
> but does not interrupt his journey by doing so.
> On the contrary, he gains new strength to finish
> it more quickly and easily since he rests only in
> order to proceed the better. (*Introduction*, part
> 2, chap. 13, p. 88)

While seemingly simple and easy to do, keeping holy thoughts is a practice whose value cannot be underestimated. In fact, St. Francis de Sales considers the use of prayerful aspirations as something absolutely essential to leading a devout life.

In what follows, we focus primarily on the aspirations and other suggestions found in the original articles of the *Spiritual Directory*, which we seek to adapt here to the realities of life in today's world.* We will also supplement the advice given in the *Directory* with instructions drawn from other writings by St.

---

* The text of the *Spiritual Directory* used in this work is based on the edition currently used by the Oblates of St. Francis de Sales. In the present work, we have generally modified the wording in two ways: by substituting a more personal form of address (e.g., "we" instead of "they") and by eliminating references that pertain specifically to life in a religious monastery.

Francis de Sales. And we will provide background information and commentary to shed further light on the meaning of the original texts. In this way, we seek to render the profound wisdom of Salesian spirituality in contemporary terms and thus to create a practical guide to the good life in the twenty-first century.

3

ON RISING:
STARTING YOUR DAY RIGHT

In his everyday spirituality, St. Francis de Sales counsels us to begin at the beginning. Making God a part of that first consciousness of the new day starts things out on the right footing. Thus, the *Spiritual Directory* opens with this exhortation:

> First of all on awakening, we are to direct our minds completely to God by some holy thought such as the following:
>
> *Sleep is the image of death and awakening that of the resurrection.*

Not merely as the first among many things to do each day, but *first of all* the devout person thinks of God, whose graceful action makes awakening possible (with the aid of an alarm clock to make it timely!). That we are alive for another day is

SALESIAN BIBLICAL INTERPRETATION

St. Francis de Sales's use of biblical quotations—which perme-ate all of his writings—reveals his thorough acquaintance with Scripture and offers a practical way by which we can appropriate the Word of God in our daily lives.* Still, despite his voluminous writing, St. Francis de Sales never published a commentary on any biblical book. His lone foray into this area was his "mystical exposition" on the Canticle of Canticles (or Song of Songs), which did not appear in print until after his death in 1622.**

By modern standards, St. Francis de Sales's interpretation of Sacred Scripture appears to be simply a personal accommodation of select verses used to support his own thoughts, or merely a literary device adopted to bolster his own ideas. But this view-point, based on today's bias in favor of critical scholarship, fails to appreciate the spiritual intelligence needed for a fuller under-standing of the Bible. That spiritual "sense" is one formed and furthered by personal experience.

---

* In his writings, St. Francis de Sales usually refers to the Vulgate edition of the Bible, a Latin translation made official by the Coun-cil of Trent (1545-1563). Because of his thorough knowledge of Sacred Scripture, he would often simply paraphrase biblical sources. For these reasons, the scriptural quotations included here may not be familiar to readers of contemporary Bible translations.

**Francis de Sales, "Mystical Exposition of the Canticle of Can-ticles," *Oeuvres* XXI:10-39. An English translation by Thomas Dailey, O.S.F.S., is available through the Salesian Center for Faith and Culture.

For St. Francis de Sales, that experience was lifelong. As Luigi Groppi rightly claims, "He has so assimilated the Sacred Bible that he possessed its language, its content, and its phrases in such a way that he used them as we do the words of our mother tongue."* Hence, the saint unabashedly tells readers of the *Introduction to the Devout Life*: "When I make use of the words of Scripture it is not always to explain them but rather to explain my own meaning by them, since they are more venerable and pleasing to devout souls" (p. 20).

Nevertheless, as Pope Pius XI attests, the Salesian approach to the Bible retains its value as offering an essential foundation for anyone's spiritual growth and development:

> In Francis' studies and especially in his interpretation of the Canticle of Canticles, many scriptural mysteries concerning moral and spiritual questions were solved; many problems were explained, and many obscure points were exposed to new light. From this it is fair to conclude that God, with an abundance of heavenly grace, enlightened the understanding of this holy man so that he might interpret the scriptures and make them understandable for both the learned and the unlearned.**

* Luigi Groppi, *Formazione teologica di S. Francesco di Sales* (Roma: Fanciulli, 1951).

**Pope Pius XI, *Urbis et Orbis*, decree proclaiming St. Francis de Sales a Doctor of the Church, July 19, 1877.

the gift each morning brings. Recognizing the source of that gift by directing our mind to do so is the appropriate response to such a gracious gift. It may take some practice, but it will prove beneficial to make this the first thought of the day, instead of reacting with annoyance or reluctance at having been awakened.

Beyond an existential awareness, the practice of directing our minds to God corresponds to and facilitates a positive psychology. Experience shows that the mood with which we begin the day tends to color the entire day. What Francis de Sales understood is that starting the day with God in mind leads to keeping God in mind throughout the day.

To fashion that mindfulness of the divine gift of our awakening each day, Francis suggests we adopt biblical images and thoughts. In this, he moves us beyond sound psychology to the adoption of a spiritual or theological understanding of the new day. Although a seemingly benign beginning to the day, the act of getting out of bed represents for St. Francis de Sales the profound reality of the resurrection and that gift of life beyond death to which we are ultimately called. To get into the habit of seeing each day as a mini resurrection is to cultivate a thoroughly Christian attitude toward our earthly existence. Thus, he suggests that when we awake:

> We may think of that voice that will ring out on the last day:
>
> *O dead, arise and come to judgment. (cf. Eph. 5:14)*

Or we may say with Job:

> I know that my Redeemer lives, and that on the
> last day I will rise again. My God, grant that this
> be to eternal glory; this hope rests in my inmost
> being. (cf. Job 19:25-26)

At other times we may say with him:

> On that day, O God, you will call me, and I will
> answer you; you will stretch forth your right arm
> to the work of your hands; you have counted all
> my steps. (cf. Job 14:15-16)

The Christian attitude with which we greet each morning is founded on faith in the Redemption and our vocation to eternal life. To cultivate this consciousness, we could recall the book of Job, that classic story of the wise man who longs to make sense of human existence amid the innocent suffering of his personal life, and who does so thanks to a divine intervention. Like Job, we can reaffirm faith in the living God and entrust ourselves to the call and care of divine providence. To do so at the beginning of the day creates a bulwark against which the travails we may encounter during the day will hold no sway.

But the tale of Job offers only one example among many possible aspirations. For this reason, the saint says:

> We should make these holy aspirations or others
> which the Holy Spirit may suggest, for we have the
> freedom to follow his inspirations.

The biblical thoughts St. Francis de Sales suggests are worthwhile words to remember and to recall, with practice, each morning. But, as he cautions here and throughout his spiritual direction, the words matter less than the affections. If we are inspired to think or speak differently by the Holy Spirit, so be it. As long as we somehow direct our mind to the Divine at day's dawning, we have begun to live today well.

But there's more with which to start our day.

> After the Angelus we will make the morning exercise, adoring our Lord from the depths of our being and thanking him for all his benefits. In union with the loving offering that the Savior made of himself to his eternal Father on the tree of the Cross, we will offer him our heart, its affections and resolutions, and our whole being, and beg for his help and blessing. We will greet our Lady and ask for her blessing, as well as that of our guardian angel and holy patrons. If we wish, we may say the Our Father. All this should be done quickly and briefly.

That may seem a lot to do *quickly and briefly*! But it can be done in the time it takes to shower or to make the morning coffee.

The brevity that the saint counsels here is an indication that, again, the saying of multiple prayers is not the primary emphasis. Rather, he recommends them here as something customary, hence, simple to do. The prayers he mentions — the Angelus, the Hail Mary, the Our Father — refer to the traditional prayers with which we grew up, prayers that are easy to remember and easy to say. Although elsewhere St. Francis de Sales emphasizes the

THE ANGELUS

(traditionally prayed at 6 a.m., noon, and 6 p.m.)

The Angel of the Lord declared to Mary:
And she conceived of the Holy Spirit.
   Hail Mary . . .
Behold the handmaid of the Lord:
Be it done unto me according to your word.
   Hail Mary . . .
And the Word was made Flesh: And dwelt among us.
   Hail Mary . . .
Pray for us, O Holy Mother of God, that we may be
made worthy of the promises of Christ.

   Let us pray: Pour forth, we beseech you, O
Lord, your grace into our hearts; that we, to whom
the incarnation of Christ, your Son, was made
known by the message of an angel, may by his
Passion and Cross be brought to the glory of his
Resurrection, through the same Christ our Lord.
Amen.

mindfulness that makes prayer effective,[40] here his point is simply
to sanctify these early moments of the day by means of thoughts
and words already familiar to us. These are the basic elements of
the morning exercise that in other spiritual traditions takes on a
more definitive and lengthier form with fixed wording.

---

[40] *Introduction*, part 2, chap. 1, p. 72: "A single Our Father said with
feeling has greater value than many said quickly and hurriedly."

In Salesian spirituality, the more important point, as always, lies in the cultivation of our heart and soul. Notice the affections the saint calls forth here: *adoring, thanking, offering,* even *begging* help and blessing. These shape the posture of the humble believer before the all-powerful God, the God who has power over life and death and who, by divine providence, has willed that this day we be alive. It is not likely that we will think such heady or heavy thoughts in the early hours of the morning, but by following the saint's suggestions we will attune ourselves to the divine gift that beckons us to begin the day.

In cultivating these affections, he urges us to recall the example of Mary (our Lady), the angels, and the saints (holy patrons), whom we can greet, or call on, with a simple "pray for us." Again, it does not seem like much, but this simple litany creates the mental reminder that we are not alone in this life, that others who lived well have gone before us, and that help for the day stands nearby.

All of this is intended to turn our morning routine into a sacred one. Routines play a key role in human life. Able to be done without our giving them much thought, they are comfortable, and often comforting, acts. Psychologically, even if not consciously, they represent a way of exercising a modicum of control over the chaos of our surroundings. Our habits lead us to do the same thing over and over again each morning; were we to deviate from this habitual routine, we would probably think something was "off" or just not right.

So, too, with the routine of praying. The words we use and the actions we perform (e.g., making the Sign of the Cross when seeing a crucifix) constitute rituals. When that routine or ritual becomes a habit — as is intended by the exercise suggested here — it creates a comfort zone in which to steady ourselves before we take on the duties of the day. Hence, even the next step in the morning routine can be made sacred:

As we begin to dress, we will make the Sign of the Cross and say:

Cover me, Lord, with the cloak of innocence and the robe of love. My God, do not let me appear before you stripped of good works.

Here the practicality of Salesian spirituality becomes obvious. Everyone gets dressed! Everyone does so automatically, without even thinking much about it (except to decide what to wear). And everyone does it every day, even when the attire is casual. Why not, then, take this daily routine and turn it into a daily prayer?

By the aspiration suggested here, we seek to "clothe" or cover ourselves with a theological sensibility. What is our Christian mission this day and every day? To live well. To live in conformity with God's will (*innocence*). To appear to others in the attire (a regal *robe*) by which a Christian is recognized and known—namely, love (or *charity*), without which we would be stripped of the good works or moral deeds that distinguish human action from that of animals.

Thus clothed with the intention to live the Faith we believe, we are ready to start our day in a grace-filled way. Now it is time to prepare for what is going to happen on this particular day.

4

ON THE DAY'S PREPARATION:
LOOKING TO BE HOLY

The mental activity described here is a shortened version of what St. Francis de Sales says of the morning exercise in his *Introduction to the Devout Life*.[41] While its five parts appear at first to be rather detailed, this exercise, too, is not intended to be painstaking or time-consuming. Rather, it can and should be done briefly, yet fervently, as a way to focus our thinking about the day that beckons.

 Since the preparation makes provision for all our actions, we will make use of it according to varying circumstances. By this means we will

---

[41] See *Introduction*, part 2, chap. 10, pp. 83-84. The exercise was originally penned as part of the "Rule of Padua" that Francis de Sales wrote for himself while a student at the university; see his *Spiritual Exercises*, pp. 26-28. Later, the founder of the Oblates of St. Francis de Sales (Blessed Louis Brisson) adapted this exercise and inserted it into the edition of the *Spiritual Directory* for use by members of his religious order.

endeavor to be disposed to carry out our activities competently and commendably.

To complete this exercise each morning takes a bit of practice. When and where we do this preparation will depend greatly on what else is going on around us (our *varying circumstances*). But no matter what these circumstances require of us, it will be possible to find a time and place to do this exercise (e.g., during the extended look in the bathroom mirror while shaving or hairstyling, or while the morning coffee is brewing). So important is this prayerful preparation that St. Francis de Sales begs readers of the *Introduction to the Devout Life* "never to omit this exercise."

Like every other aspect of getting ready in the morning, this exercise has an eminently practical purpose — namely, to help us do well those things that we have to do anyhow! That is why life coaches, leadership gurus, and spiritual masters of varying traditions all recommend the conscious consideration of our daily duties and responsibilities as the best place to start on the quest to become the person we want to be.

In the Salesian tradition, that consideration necessarily includes God, which makes this morning exercise more than just a highly successful but secular habit (e.g., in the mold of Steven Covey enterprises). The Salesian preparation is decidedly spiritual, because it "makes provision for all [our] actions" not only as entries on a calendar but as expressions of God's will for us during this particular day. It renders the entirety of our day as consisting of occasions for the practice of virtue, and thus *commendable* activities for which we need to be *competent* in a spiritual way.

The Salesian preparation of the day is really a prayer—perhaps the only time in a busy day that we may have to pray! Here's how it works:

STEP 1: INVOCATION

We will invoke the help of God, saying:

> *Lord, if you do not care for my soul, it is useless that another should do so. (Ps 127:1)*

We will ask him to make us worthy to spend the day with him without offending him. For this purpose, the words of the psalm may be helpful:

> *Teach me to do your will, for you are my God. Your good spirit will guide me by the hand on level ground (Ps. 143:10), and your divine majesty by its inexpressible love and boundless charity will give me true life.*

As with all things spiritual, we begin by asking for divine grace to help us. Doing so situates the exercise in its rightful realm as prayer and not merely planning. We make this prayer by acknowledging God's benevolent providence: his "care for my soul," his "good spirit," his "boundless charity"—all expressed with personal regard for me and my life. In response to this divine goodness toward us, we put our entire day into a transcendent context and intend to spend the day faithfully with God, in and through the immanent things we have to do. Envisioning what those things are constitutes the next step.

LIVING BETWEEN
THE TWO WILLS OF GOD*

Each day offers numerous possibilities for living well. For St. Francis de Sales, how we respond to these opportunities is our way of living "between" the two wills of God.

The one is God's "signified will" and includes "the truths which God wills that we should believe, the goods he will have us hope for, the pains he will have us dread, what he will have us love, the commandments he will have us observe, and the counsels he desires us to follow" (*Treatise*, book 8, chap. 3, pp. 329-330). These are the dimensions of daily life made known to us by more or less explicit means. We know God's will as it is told to us outright in Sacred Scripture, whether stated as law (e.g., the Commandments) or counseled as wise (e.g., the Beatitudes) or promoted as virtuous (e.g., the evangelical counsels of chastity, poverty, and obedience). We know the divine will, too, through the explicit teaching of those commissioned by God to teach it (i.e., the Church's Magisterium). And we can also know God's will with clarity through the laws that natures teaches us. To submit to these various manifestations of God's will is one way in which we love God.

---

* See also the introduction by Wendy Wright and Joseph Power in *Letters of Spiritual Direction*, pp. 40-43 and Wendy Wright's keynote address on "Seeking God's Will Together: Discernment in the Salesian World of Hearts," given at the quadrennial convocation of the Wilmington-Philadelphia province of the Oblates of St. Francis de Sales (June 2003).

The other is a love that accepts God's "good pleasure," which summarily refers to any and all things that happen to us but are not brought about by us. Whether comforting or afflicting, pleasurable or painful, the daily events of our lives "show us, by their very happening, that God has willed and intended them" (*Treatise*, book 9, chap. 1, p. 365). In particular, the saint has in mind those inexplicable ways in which we might suffer due to no fault of our own. To accept these unwanted but often inevitable trials for the love of God, he says, is the high point of charity, because our human nature inclines us to avoid or reject them. But in the Salesian perspective, those very things we may consider negative, painful, or even unjust are also happenings that take place in accord with God's providence. And since God can will only what is good for us, those things, too, are given to us ultimately for our benefit.

STEP 2: FORESIGHT

This is simply a preview or conjecture of all that could happen during the course of the day. Thus, with the grace of Our Lord, we will wisely and prudently anticipate occasions which could take us by surprise.

Taking a mental glance at the day's calendar, we *preview* what awaits us in terms of places to go and things to do and people to see. Here we activate the insightfulness of Salesian spirituality—namely, that the responsibilities of our personal vocation constitute the real place where we act out the devout life.

But this conjecture involves more than simply pondering our to-do list for the day. As an act of prayer, this foresight considers our daily tasks as occasions for living out our Faith or, conversely, as occasions that might tempt us to do otherwise. In the familiar words of corporate strategic planning, we envision "opportunities" and "threats," but here they are to be considered in terms of our being a disciple of the Lord this day. To live that discipleship well, we take the next step.

STEP 3: PLAN OF ACTION

> We will carefully plan and seek out the best means to avoid any faults. We will also arrange in an orderly fashion what, in our opinion, is proper for us to do.

Each day, indeed all of human life, is fraught with temptations, and we all have our faults. In this intersection of the secular and the personal, we come up against roadblocks to devotion, potential obstacles to living a life of charity carefully, frequently, and promptly. In the Salesian planning process, we deal with these first.

If we can foresee problematic situations we are likely to face at some point in the day, we can better prepare "to avoid any faults" there and instead to respond as God would have us do. Perhaps we will encounter someone we know to be annoying. Perhaps we will be especially challenged by some task. Perhaps we will have to endure something particularly trying. Each of these moments in our day holds the possibility of vice or virtue, which is why determining how we will respond requires careful planning on our part. The goal here is to envision these episodes ahead of time so as not to be caught off guard when they happen.

Thus readied for any temptations that may threaten our devotion, we should also prepare for those potentially positive opportunities to serve God well. In all these considerations, we simply put into our minds an idea about how we should or should not act. Whether our plans come to fruition is another story! But as the day begins, we make it our intention to avoid vice and to practice virtue—not in general, but according to the concrete situations that actually await us. That intention is the foundation of the next step.

STEP 4: RESOLUTION

We will make a firm resolution to obey the will of God, especially during the present day. To this end, we will use the words of the royal prophet David:

My soul, will you not cheerfully obey the holy will of God, seeing that your salvation comes from him? (Ps. 62:2)

Surely this God of infinite majesty and admittedly worthy of every honor and service can only be neglected by us through a lack of courage. Let us, therefore, be consoled and strengthened by this beautiful verse of the psalmist:

> *Let evil men do their worst against me. The Lord,*
> *the king, can overcome them all. Let the world*
> *complain about me to its heart's content. This*
> *means little to me because he who holds sway over*
> *all the angelic spirits is my protector. (Ps. 99:1)*

To be effective, the foregoing considerations of how to live this day well cannot be mere data points or calendar entries. Here, the practical dimension of Salesian spirituality emphasizes the need to move beyond knowledge into the realm of the will. Our actions arise from our choices and decisions, which ultimately are what will make us into the persons we desire to become.

Thus, the saint exhorts us to "resolve firmly" to live according to God's will. Making a resolution is all we can do at this point, since the day's activities are still in the future. But resolve we must; otherwise, our preparation remains nothing but nice ideas or hopeful wishes.

To make a resolution is to make a decision, and decisions get us going. To go in the right direction, we align our decisions with what we have come to see as God's holy will for us this day. After all, if the destination of our devotion (and our life) is union with God, we begin to reach that eternal objective by uniting ourselves to the divine will in the human reality of the present. This we can do *cheerfully*! The day will still have its challenges, to be sure. But by bringing faith to the responsibilities we have to face this day, we can be consoled and strengthened, knowing that a loving and merciful God remains at our side.

But before we set foot out the door, one final step remains.

STEP 5: RECOMMENDATION

 We will entrust ourselves and all our concerns into the hands of God's eternal goodness and ask him to consider us as always so commended. Leaving to him the complete care of what we are and what he wants us to be, we will say with all our heart:

> *I have asked you one thing, O Jesus, my Lord, and I shall ask you again and again, namely, that I may faithfully carry out your loving will all the days of my poor and pitiable life. (Ps. 27:4; 40:9)*

> *I commend to you, O gracious Lord, my soul, my life, my heart, my memory, my understanding, and my will. Grant that in and with all these, I may serve you, love you, please and honor you forever. (Ps. 31:6; Luke 23:46)*

Entrusting ourselves — this is the final step because it is the ultimate act of faith. We have done all that we could do at this point (preparing and resolving). Now we recognize that all our concerns are best left in bigger hands, hands whose providential power knows no limit, whose mercy envelops us with "complete care." We cast ourselves into God's loving grasp with regard to our personal identity ("who we are") and our vocational destiny ("what he wants us to be"). The verses of the psalm, or whatever aspiration we choose to use, serve both to effect this recommendation (a prayer) and to provide confidence (a grace) as we now begin the day.

5

ON THE DIRECTION OF INTENTION:
THE KEY TO SPIRITUAL PERFECTION

Having prepared ourselves to face the day with God's grace, it now begins. But before explaining in detail how our various duties are moments in which to encounter God, St. Francis de Sales offers his keen insight into how any and every human activity can become a supernatural experience. In fact, this little exercise — the Direction of Intention[42] — is the Salesian key to unlocking the devout life.

If we wish to thrive and advance in the way of our Lord, we should, at the beginning of our actions, both exterior and interior, ask for his grace and offer to his divine Goodness all the

---

[42] As Fr. Balducelli notes in his commentary (chap. 5, page 1), the title "Direction of Intention" is customary but not totally accurate. It might better be called "the rightness of intention"

good we will do. In this way we will be prepared to bear with peace and serenity all the pain and suffering we will encounter as coming from the fatherly hand of our good God and Savior. His most holy intention is to have us merit by such means in order to reward us afterward out of the abundance of his love.

We should not neglect this practice in matters which are small and seemingly insignificant, nor even if we are engaged in those things which are agreeable and in complete conformity with our own will and needs, such as drinking, eating, resting, recreating and similar actions. By [our] following the advice of St. Paul the Apostle (cf. 1 Cor. 10:31; Col. 3:17), everything we do will be done in God's name to please him alone.

On its face, the Direction of Intention is a simple prayer, uttered briefly at the outset of whatever we are about to do. On further reflection, however, this single exercise encapsulates and reveals the spiritual genius of St. Francis de Sales, for it incorporates his anthropological vision, his theological sensibility, and his psychological intuition.

Anthropologically, the Direction of Intention is predicated on the tenets of a fully Christian humanism. In this worldview, we have been purposefully created by God. We come from love (because our existence is neither necessary nor useful to the

---

(i.e., what should be impressed on us) or, better still, "the right intending of deeds" (i.e., giving to our actions a new spiritual paradigm).

eternally all-perfect God), and we are made for love (in spousal union, neighborly charity, and divine communion). To live "in the image and likeness of God" is, therefore, to love, and for St. Francis de Sales this entails both thinking (consciousness) and deciding (willingness). As such, living well means attending specifically to these personal dimensions of life because our actions reveal who we are and how we love (or do not love).

The Direction of Intention provides this attention by creating in us a new spiritual habit—the habit of asking and offering and accepting before doing. By first directing the intention with which we act, we address what we do to God, whom we love.[43] By fashioning our deeds in this way, we render indifferent acts good (rather than merely circumstantial) and good deeds even better (by adding a positive motivation).

Theologically, this is how we participate in the divine work of salvation. As with Mary's fiat after listening to the angel Gabriel's announcement of her divine maternity—"let it be [done] to me according to your word" (Luke 1:38)—holiness begins with the grace of God but also calls for the free act of human cooperation. If, as we believe, the Incarnation brings God's saving presence to human life, and if God's divinity incarnate in Jesus is to become incarnate in us,[44] then we must live this event

---

[43] Concerning the intention, Francis de Sales uses the French verb *dresser*, "to tend to, to fashion, to process." In his "Commentary" (chap. 5, page 2), Fr. Balducelli explains that "this is precisely what the precept prescribes. Instead of letting intentions just emerge from spontaneities and drives, we are told to attend to them, to tutor and fashion them, to process them, as it were, so that the normative paradigm for intending be mirrored in them."

[44] Cf. Wendy Wright, "Birthing Jesus: A Salesian Understanding of Christian Life," *Studia Mystica* 13/1 (March 1990): 23-44.

SALESIAN ANTHROPOLOGY*

The central role that intentionality plays in the good life is predicated on a distinct understanding of the human condition and the spiritual life. St. Francis de Sales believes the human being to be a microcosm (*Treatise*, book 10, chap. 1). Made of body and soul, flesh and spirit, each person represents the perfection of the universe in the embodiment of what is both angelic and animal, spiritual and physical.

Moved by passions (based on sense knowledge) and affections (based on reasoning), each of us is drawn to act according to whom or what we love. The good life, then, "does not consist in the absence but in the regulation of the passions"; because these interior movements "are to our heart what strings are to a lute," they need to be tuned regularly so as to be in harmony (*Oeuvres*, vol. 8, p. 355; cf. *Introduction*, part 5, chap. 7). That need for self-regulation reflects the tension within us between the inferior part of our souls, with which we naturally seek gratification and avoid pain, and the superior part, by which we focus on what we ought to do as right and good even at the cost of experiencing pain.

Ultimately, the choice is ours: to become, with the help of divine grace, more like God or to follow the attraction of something else that claims our love. Hence, intentionality — which

---

* See James Langelaan, *The Philosophy and Theology of Love according to St. Francis de Sales* [Toronto Studies in Theology, vol. 67] (Lampeter, UK: Edwin Mellen Press, 1994), pp. 10-20.

integrates affections, understanding, and free will—is the vehicle for becoming who we are.

And intentionality operates within the human heart. As Wendy Wright and Joseph Power explain:

> At the root of [Francis de Sales's] perception, and at the deepest point of wisdom of Salesian spirituality, is the assumption … that the spiritual life is not primarily about understanding, nor solely a matter of enthusiasm. It is a dynamic, integrative process that is brought about through the engagement of the whole person. The heart in Salesian thought is the seat both of intellect and of will. There the affective as well as cognitive capacities of the person are seen to dwell. All Salesian praxis then proceeds from this conceptual point of departure. (*Letters of Spiritual Direction*, pp. 57-58)

consciously and meaningfully through the choices we make. As Fr. Roger Balducelli puts it, "The direction of intention is one way in which this kind of lived-through transformation can be made to happen. By reintending in relation to God the deeds we do, we divinize our deeds, as it were, and in that sense we make the Incarnation-event happen within our own history" ("Commentary," chap. 5, p. 4).

This divinization and sanctification apply to every aspect of human life. Each day we find ourselves facing a myriad of things to do. Some we plan ahead for, others we just list, and most we simply act on. With so many things calling for our attention, we often run the risk of *doing* more than *being*.

For this reason, St. Francis de Sales counsels us to pause, ever so briefly, before anything we do and make a threefold prayer in which we ask for God's grace, offer to God the action we are about to do, and promise to accept whatever will happen in the process. The prayer is not complicated, difficult, or time-consuming. But psychologically it holds the power to transform our lives completely.

First, we ask for God's grace. This brief petition does more than plead for help. It situates us and our activity in a transcendent context. Asking shifts the focus of our attention away from ourselves and our natural self-centeredness. Asking for help confesses our inadequacy at being the masters of existence. Asking for help from God professes the supremacy of the divine in our lives. Making this spiritual plea at the outset of our activity serves to reorient our thinking (and thus our acting) toward God, with whom we seek to be united, now and forever.

This request for divine assistance reveals a "sacramental" view of the world. By imploring God's help, we disavow our self-sufficiency and express confidence that divine grace is necessary for all we do. According to Fr. Balducelli:

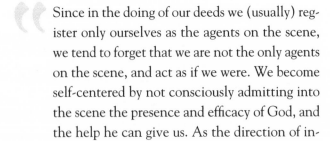

> Since in the doing of our deeds we (usually) register only ourselves as the agents on the scene, we tend to forget that we are not the only agents on the scene, and act as if we were. We become self-centered by not consciously admitting into the scene the presence and efficacy of God, and the help he can give us. As the direction of intention prescribes that we should ask for God's

grace, it remedies our forgetfulness of God, and heals the self-centeredness that feeds on that forgetfulness. ("Commentary," chap. 5, p. 12)

Next, we offer to God all the good we will do. Offering is a selfless act. It situates our activity in a context that transcends only ourselves. Offering our good deeds to another preserves us from the false and engrossing illusion that what we do here and now is of absolute value. Offering the good we do to God reminds us that the immediacy of our concerns for ourselves, our work, and our place in this world are far and away surpassed by the absolute goodness of God. Moreover, by intending to do what we do not for our sake but for God's, we trade the pleasure principle (acting out of self-interest) for a generosity principle (acting for the good of another). When we adopt this principle and direct what we are to do toward God, something natural becomes supernatural.

This act of offering reflects a "liturgical" view of the world. We offer what we have, what we do, and who we are—and in the process our deeds become everyday acts of worship. That makes our faith something greater than an occasional exercise, what Fr. Balducelli calls the "intermittent religion" of one who relates to God "only when duty calls, or when emergencies ... make it imperative, or when the solemnity of the occasion makes it inevitable" ("Commentary," chap. 5, p. 10). Instead, the re-intending of all our deeds helps us to achieve and sustain our relatedness to God at every moment of the day.

Finally, we promise to accept whatever may come and *bear with* whatever may happen, even if this entails pain and suffering. By professing humility at the outset and offering our work to God, we do the only things we can do. We cannot control circumstances. We cannot determine outcomes. But we can lessen any frantic concerns about what may or may not happen around us by entrusting all that we do into "the fatherly hand of our good God and Savior."

This act of abandonment puts into practice a "providential" view of the world. If we really believe that God desires our eternal happiness, then all that we do (successfully or not) and all that happens to us (happily or not) pertains to a divine design. Our part is simply to do what we can—and do so for love of God, who never ceases to care for us. And when we do this, as Fr. Balducelli points out, "when the hurtful is allowed for, and accepted in advance, the advent of it hurts only superficially." As a result, "the state of peace in which the self is established will not be disestablished by any momentary skirmish with adversity" ("Commentary," chap. 5, p. 6).

By way of example, consider how the Direction of Intention can be applied to a common task: the daily commute. Regardless of the destination or duration or means of transportation, most of us take part in some daily commute. Before setting out on our way, we ask for God's grace. In that way, we begin our trek conscious of God's presence. Then we offer to God whatever good may come from the commute. The principal good, of course, is getting where we need to go. But other goods may accompany us on our trip. Perhaps we will see beauty along the way. Perhaps we will have an opportunity to grow in virtue (such as patience!). Perhaps we will discover something new. In any case, whatever happens, we have already decided to experience it as a gift and in gratitude offer it back to the divine Source of all good gifts. But other things may also happen. Traffic jams may occur. Other drivers may annoy us. We may even end up being late. Nevertheless, having allowed for them ahead of time, these "momentary skirmishes" do not and cannot deter us from the ultimate task of being united with God along the way. Approaching our commute in this way will necessarily give it an entirely different character. Practicing the right intending of our commute this way every day adds up to an altogether new way of traveling — and of living well as we go.

Asking, offering, and accepting — this spiritual triad constitutes the heart of Salesian asceticism "if we wish to thrive and advance in the way of the Lord." For St. Francis de Sales, living well depends not on positive circumstances or successful outcomes but only on the grace-filled transformation that occurs "from the inside out." It calls not for bodily discipline or physical mortification, but for a new consciousness and a new willingness, a metanoia of the mind and conversion of the heart. It entails the habitual practice of reintending what we do for love of God, who enables us to do everything we do. In this, it generates a transfiguration of who we are into what God has called us to be.

Best of all, this directing of our intention can be applied to everything we do. The deed itself is not decisive. Whether small or great, extraordinary or run-of-the-mill, necessary or optional — all our activities can be divinized, can be "done in God's name to please him alone." Even actions that fulfill basic human needs — such as drinking, eating, and resting — can be made pleasing to God by our humbly asking for God's grace, generously offering what is good about them to God, and trustingly accepting whatever happens as a result.

In the Salesian tradition, intentionality is the lynchpin to living well. It goes to the heart of who we are as conscious, willing persons. It gives focus to what we do as imperfect people trying to accomplish good. It renders meaningful the many moments of life by locating their significance in the arc of eternity, where the ultimate source of value is the divine source of our present being and our future becoming.

Thus, in whatever we do, if we learn to direct our intention to the fulfillment of God's will, our actions can never fail, no matter what the results may be. If our aim is to please God, then we do! And every day we start all over again, knowing that we are one day closer to our eternal salvation.

6

ON MEALS:
FINDING THE EXTRAORDINARY IN THE ORDINARY

Keeping in mind the guiding principle of reintending our deeds, we now set out on the day's journey. There we regularly come across many common moments that can be divinized, from the labors of our work (even at home) to the downtime of our leisure. But St. Francis de Sales begins his guide to the good life with a basic need of any life — nourishment.

The notion behind the article on meals is simple. In its original form, it presumes the custom of having all the Sisters gather in the refectory at established times for meals. But it begins by noting how even this exercise can be ordered in a spiritual sense:

> We should not go merely to eat, but to obey God and to take part in shared experience of community with one another.

Here we see the everydayness of Salesian spirituality. Whether it is a short break in the routine of work or a prepared meal with the family at home, the quotidian task of eating represents an opportunity to live well. Recognizing it as such entails envisioning the event as an opportunity to obey God rather than simply to consume food.

Most of us probably do not consider mealtime in this light. At its basest level, eating is simply how we obtain the caloric energy we need to satisfy our hunger and move on with the day. Given our hectic calendars, mealtime nowadays also tends to be work time, as, for example, when we schedule a meeting with clients over a meal or when we try to get something else done while we are eating. Concerned with maximizing our time, we focus not on food or its consumption, but on matters that may actually contribute to our indigestion!

This is why the saintly Doctor prescribes a reintending of what we do when we dine. It is an ordinary event, but it holds extraordinary potential. These moments of the day are not merely times to eat. They represent times to live well with God, who has created us in such a way that we must eat (to survive) and we must do so repeatedly and regularly (to feel well). This attentiveness to our natural need is therefore an act of obedience to the Creator, who made us to be hungry.

Mealtime also represents an opportunity to relate to others. Sadly, this relationality no longer holds sway when people, especially family members, give priority to other things that prevent coming together to share a meal. Still, when we do gather at table with others, their presence is something to which we should be attuned.

Once our intention to eat is redirected toward this experience of loving God and one another, St. Francis de Sales suggests that we also attend to how we eat. Here he considers two aspects of eating that we all experience at one time or another—the tendency to be too picky or to be too indulgent.

> If we tend to be too particular or too eager in eating, we should, upon entering the place, make a firm resolution and invoke the grace and help of Our Lord to courageously exercise self-control. Let the one who is too particular consider the gall offered to Our Lord at the height of his bitterest sufferings. Let the one who is too eager think of the abstinence and strict fasts of the Fathers of the desert and of so many other saints who so effectively mortified their appetite.

An honest acknowledgment of our inner attitude—whether we are too particular or too eager—leads us to "invoke the grace and help of Our Lord" to make this particular meal an occasion for practicing the virtue of self-control. This request for divine assistance we can make in the silence of our grace before the meal.

As an exercise in transforming our consciousness with regard to this event, St. Francis de Sales invites us to think of the holy example of others, such as our Lord when he suffered thirst on the Cross; the desert Fathers, whose austere lives did not allow for sumptuous feasts; or any of the other saints who disciplined their appetite by choosing to abstain from food and drink at various times in their storied lives. None of these had the luxury of being finicky eaters. Considering how many people in the world suffer due to a lack of food, our gratefulness for what we have to eat ought to outweigh the extremes of our refusal to eat something or our gluttony in eating anything too eagerly.

In addition, mealtime gives us the chance to practice another spiritual discipline:

> We should never leave the table without having denied ourselves in some way. Nevertheless, we ought to eat without hesitation or objection any foods given us for our well-being. With a spirit of indifference we are to accept from the hand of the Lord what we like as well as what we do not like, be it food or anything else.

In this dual practice of self-denial and non-denial, we see the distinctive approach of Salesian spirituality, a steady and moderate one that the saint prefers because it "doesn't show in public, bothers no one, and is well adapted to social life" (*Introduction*, part 3, chap. 23, p. 174).

The practice of denying ourselves in some way at table reminds us that our personal instincts and existential needs do not control our freedom. Instead, we can choose to forgo some delectable delight, such as a favorite condiment or a tempting dessert or even a second helping. In this way, we can exercise a bit of mastery over our senses and thus give priority to the spirit over the flesh.

By eating what is set before us "without hesitation or objection," we acknowledge what we have as a gift (even if we pay for it in a restaurant!) and recognize food as something provided for our well-being ultimately by the Giver of all good gifts. Thus, to accept our portion without choice and without complaint is to reconfigure our act of eating in such a way that food is no longer

THE CUSTOM OF FASTING*

The practice of abstaining from food has long been a staple of Christian piety. Based on Sacred Scripture and the Church Fathers, fasting is one of the three traditional forms of penance (the others being prayer and almsgiving) that, according to the *Catechism of the Catholic Church*, seek to "help us acquire mastery over our instincts and freedom of heart" (no. 2043). In Roman Catholicism, fasting is also to be observed as preparation for the worthy reception of the Eucharist.

While St. Francis de Sales recognizes and commends the disciplinary value of fasting, his approach to this and other bodily mortifications in the *Introduction* takes greater account of the heart of the person than of the type of exterior action. He perceives the risk that fasting can be counterproductive when it is undertaken with austerity or without regard for one's health: "We are very much exposed to temptation both when our bodies are too pampered and when too run down, for the one makes the body demanding in its softened state and the other desperate with affliction" (p. 173).

Instead, he counsels a more practical approach, based on the principle that "steady, moderate sobriety is preferable to periods of violent abstinence, interspersed with periods of great self-indulgence" (p. 174). By teaching us to eat what is set before us, whether it is in keeping with our tastes or not, the saint focuses our self-discipline not on food, or the lack thereof, but on the

---

* See *Introduction to the Devout Life*, part 3, chap. 23, pp. 172-176.

choices we make and the attitudes we bring to the table. As he pointedly observes, "To set one kind of food aside in order to eat another kind, examine and criticize everything, find nothing properly prepared or good enough, and make a to-do over every mouthful, all this reveals a soft character attached to dishes and dainties" (p. 174).

If, on the other hand, we learn to "renounce not only our taste but our choice as well" (p. 174), we do more to correct our hearts than to punish our bodies. And this interior conversion remains paramount, for "since the heart is the source of our actions, as the heart is, so are they" (p. 172).

simply the satisfaction of a natural desire but the reception of a supernatural gift.

For St. Francis de Sales, this "spirit of indifference" actually represents the high point of living well, which is why he applies it to "food or anything else." By *indifference* here, he does not mean an uncaring attitude about what we ingest. Rather, a holy indifference is one that subjugates a personal desire for something we want and instead accepts what is providentially given to us. *Indifference*, in this sense, does not mean that we do not care but that we care so much to do what God wills, it does not matter whether we like it or not. Adopting this attitude in the relatively small matter of what we eat gives us good practice in making it an approach to greater things (good or bad) that we are given in life.

In the Salesian tradition, this daily exercise at mealtime expresses in practical terms a deeper spiritual dimension to life. St.

Francis de Sales's gastronomic counsel arises from his theological understanding of obedience to God's will as it is communicated in one (or both) of two ways—through his signified will and his good pleasure—throughout our lives, as explained earlier (see "Living between the Two Wills of God," p. 60).

On the one hand, the satisfying of our natural need to eat reflects one way in which we respond to God's signified will. Eating is something we naturally have to do; but this "law" is built into our lives by the Creator of all life. Hence, by choosing to do what we must do anyhow, we give a supernatural impetus to what is a natural necessity. We do what we must because hunger signifies that this is the divine will for us.

On the other hand, by ingesting our food indifferently (neither complaining nor overindulging), our eating expresses our willingness to conform to God's good pleasure. The food we receive, whether it be tasty or not, is a gift from God's providential hand. We may not particularly care for it or choose to order it when we dine out. But if we look on it as a divine gift, we can accept it willingly and thereby transcend our self-interest.

The fact of eating may be a creaturely necessity. The delight of eating may be a matter of taste. But by reintending the meal as a spiritual exercise, what seems merely dietary can be divine. If we can learn to approach eating a meal as an opportunity to obey God and share goodness with others, this ordinary act becomes something extraordinary, and part of a daily routine for living well.

7

ON WORK:
AND TAKING
SPIRITUAL REPOSE

The lengthiest part of almost everyone's day is taken up with work, however that comes to be defined. It might be a salaried job or volunteer service. It might be something we go to or something we do at home. It might happen during bankers' hours or the night shift or sometime in between. It might involve a white-collar profession or blue-collar labor or some other color-coded category of work. But whatever our job is, it usually requires the greater amount of our time each day.

That is precisely why St. Francis de Sales offers us exercises to focus our attention during this part of the day so as to transform time at work into an opportunity to lead a good life. Although cloistered nuns have a different sense and purpose for their labor,[45] the advice the saint gives in the *Spiritual Directory* can be applied to any work situation.

---

[45] In the context of the monastic life, work is undertaken in silence. The tasks to be performed (e.g., cooking, cleaning, gardening, et cetera) are such that during this quiet time the Sisters could

> On entering the place of work, we should place ourselves in the presence of God, asking for his grace to make use of this time in accordance with the holy purpose for which it was instituted.

Work is our lot in life, as the biblical book of Genesis makes clear. We have been empowered by the Creator to do work (Gen. 1:26-28), and from the beginning of time it has been part of our earthly existence, as we see in the biblical tale of Adam and Eve tilling the Garden of Eden and caring for it (Gen. 2:15). Although it may be burdensome and accompanied by frustration (Gen. 3:17-19), work precedes sin in the order of creation and thus should not be seen as a punishment. Whatever its particular character, work is part and parcel of our human vocation.

With this humanistic vision of work in mind, St. Francis de Sales counsels us to begin our working day with the now familiar direction of intention, by recognizing that wherever we work, we are in the presence of God and asking for grace to work well this day. This simple prayer, uttered at the beginning of our work, shifts the focus from the job that awaits us to "the holy purpose for which it was instituted"—namely, the sanctification of the worker in the plan of the Creator.

---

continue their contemplation, which is their primary work. For this reason, the original *Spiritual Directory* presupposes a prior time of prayer and includes several suggestions on how the Sisters "may make use of their meditation, looking on Our Lord in the mystery which they considered and dwelling on certain points they particularly appreciated." These details have been omitted here, although the principle of bringing God to mind while we work remains.

When we begin our work, we should say interiorly: "Speak, Lord, your servant is listening" (1 Sam. 3:9-10). O my God, make me worthy to accomplish your holy will.

This aspiration creates prayerfulness in the workplace. Beginning in this way, we are able to transcend the mundane materiality of what we have to do. This brief interior act sets our labors within the prospect of listening to God, who calls us to our tasks. Our work then becomes an expression of obedience in accomplishing the divine will.

Now, ready to knuckle down to accomplish the tasks at hand, we can also benefit from attuning ourselves to God's continuing presence while we work. To do this, St. Francis de Sales counsels the use of silence, consideration, and imagination. These acts enable us to make a little spiritual retreat during the day, which the saint characterizes elsewhere as "one of the most certain means to spiritual advancement" (*Introduction*, part 2, chap. 12, p. 85).

First, there are likely times during our work, whatever it might be, in which we labor in silence. We can transform these times into precious moments by being quiet on the inside as well.

The purpose of silence is not only the prevention of idle chatter, but also the curtailing of wandering and useless thoughts while speaking with God, and the obtaining of new strength to work unceasingly in divine service.

When we habituate ourselves to thinking of God while completing our tasks (and even *speaking with* God, although not out loud), we maintain that supernatural focus with which we began to work. This focus opens the door to grace, which gives strength for working well as a service to God, who has given us our many abilities.

Beyond that momentary silence, we might also enjoy a more extended spiritual retreat. This assumes that we can steal some time away from our labors, however briefly, during which we can think and retreat into our inner world. Although some tasks require undivided attention (the work of a surgeon, for example), for the most part our work affords us opportunities to take some sort of break, even if only in our minds.[46] And in those nonworking moments, we can cultivate the spiritual life, as St. Francis de Sales points out:

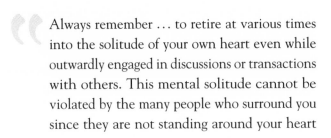

> Always remember ... to retire at various times into the solitude of your own heart even while outwardly engaged in discussions or transactions with others. This mental solitude cannot be violated by the many people who surround you since they are not standing around your heart

[46] St. Francis de Sales elsewhere suggests the practice of a parallel "spiritual repose" akin to the siesta common in European cultures. He calls this "sacred sleep" a time in which he will consider: (1) the good experiences that God has inspired, (2) the vanity of this world's pleasures, (3) the misery of vice and sin, (4) the excellence of virtue, (5) the gift of human intelligence, (6) the rigor of divine justice, (7) the wonderful attributes of God, and (8) the eternal goodness of God's love (*Spiritual Exercises*, pp. 33-36).

but only around your body. Your heart remains alone in the presence of God.... Indeed, our tasks are seldom so important as to keep us from withdrawing our hearts from them from time to time in order to retire into this divine solitude. (*Introduction*, part 2, chap. 12, p. 86)

During this mental (if not also physical) break, the saint suggests we reenergize by refocusing our thoughts so as to become more conscious of developing ourselves as workers and thus to "be who we are and be that well." To this end, he counsels us to use our imagination to paint a picture that will aid us in what we are doing.

If we suffer from some strong temptation or emotion, we can find courage and strength in considering the pains of Our Lord, picturing him undergoing them. When we experience difficulty in the practice of virtues, we will be enlightened and aided if we consider Him in the exercise of those virtues which He practiced while on earth.

In the Salesian tradition, imaginative considerations give us the ability to pray while we work — without leaving where we are. By bringing God to mind, we bring the divine into ourselves. As Jesus suffered pains with courage, so can we find strength to do so; as Jesus practiced virtue every day, so can we be enlightened to see how to do so. This thought exercise takes little time but has an exceptional power to produce salutary effects in us and, by extension, to transform positively the work we do.

THE SALESIAN IMAGINATION*

Perhaps more so than any author of his time, St. Francis de Sales makes extensive use of the imagination. His writings contain numerous images (thirty-three thousand, by one count!) that give to his work a literary power to convey spiritual truths clearly, creatively, and eloquently. But for this saint, the imagination also has a productive power that is decidedly personal. In his view, the forming of mental images, under the inspiration of the Holy Spirit, has "an inestimable efficacy to enlighten the mind and move the will" (*On the Preacher and Preaching*, p. 50). Cultivating this unique human faculty is a chief means for bringing about our continual conversion toward God.

In Salesian spirituality, using one's imagination produces an awareness of God's presence in our lives. As the saint explains: "Although faith assures us of his presence, yet because we do not see him with our eyes we often forget about him and behave as if God were far distant from us. We really know that he is present, but because we do not reflect on that fact we act as if we did not know it" (*Introduction*, part 2, chap. 2, p. 74). Thus, in order to pray at any time or in any place, all we need to do is imagine the reality of what we believe, that God remains always with us.

---

* See T. Dailey, "Playful Prayer: Imagination and the Task of Theology in Salesian Perspective," in William Ruhl, ed., *Salesian Spirituality: Catalyst to Collaboration* (Washington, DC: De Sales School of Theology, 1993), pp. 169-188. Cf. John D. Lyons, *Before Imagination: Embodied Thought from Montaigne to Rousseau* (Stanford, CA: Stanford University Press, 2005), pp. 61-93.

Our imagination is also beneficial in its power to excite within us those considerations and affections that motivate us to lead better lives. By imaginatively portraying God as gazing down on us from heaven or standing alongside us, we are likely to act differently. By picturing ourselves as the subjects in a Gospel story, we more vividly hear Jesus' words or feel the effects of his touch or see the wonders of his power; and in this we experience the grace of divine revelation that empowers us to know the truth more fully, to show goodness through mercy, or to praise the beauty of the world around us.

Through the practice of spiritual time management we are able to turn the workday into yet another way to live well. Given how much time we spend "on the job," learning to manage it spiritually helps us profit by it in terms of our eternal vocation. St. Francis de Sales's final piece of advice on the topic of work focuses on this dimension of time and our spiritual imagination.

> At each hour of the day, let us regret hours wasted and recall that we will have to give an account of this hour and all the moments of our life. Let us remember that we are approaching eternity, that hours are centuries to the damned, that we are running toward death, and that perhaps our last hour may soon be at hand.

Admittedly, this sounds a bit dire, but it certainly is true. Time flies—and does so in only one direction! Thus, with each passing hour of the day (which, in a Visitation monastery, is recalled with the tolling of a bell), we draw closer to eternity. And although the exact time remains unknown, and may even be "soon at hand," our date with that destiny is undeniable.

This bit of realism is not intended to be frightening. Rather, the saint counsels us to embrace this truth confidently[47] and allow it to set us free for living well during the time we have.

> After such thoughts [about the end of time], we should make devout aspirations that God be merciful to us at that last hour. This will certainly happen for those who have been very faithful in doing this. By this means we will grow and progress daily from virtue to virtue, even to the perfection of divine love.

Here the optimism that characterizes Salesian spirituality is most evident. If, at each hour of the day, we call upon the mercy of God, we cultivate a vibrant sense of humility and docility that allows the grace of salvation to take ever greater root in our lives. Recognizing our need for God's mercy reintegrates the Redemption within us. Doing this as often as hourly *perfects* that divine love throughout the course of our day and, consequently, throughout our lives.

[47] The positive dimension to this spiritual strategy is evident in the powerful "meditation on death" that St. Francis includes in his *Introduction to the Devout Life*, part 1, chap. 13, pp. 49-50.

By practicing these spiritual exercises while we labor, the real work that takes up each day becomes not simply the accomplishment of secular tasks but the sanctification of who we are, in view of the eternal work of salvation that God has worked for us.

8

ON LEISURE:
INTERACTING WITH OTHERS

Work may be our lot in life, but there's more to our day than our labors. What we do after hours also plays a significant role in living well. Many treat this as "free" time, in the sense of a time in which we have no other obligations. But for St. Francis de Sales, the call to "be who we are and be that well" takes no time off. Thus, even free time offers an opportunity to grow in virtue and become who God calls us to be.

For the Sisters of the Visitation, St. Francis de Sales penned advice about this under the rubric of recreation. Admittedly, what this means for monastic life and for modern society are markedly different.[48] Nevertheless, the exercises he suggests

---

[48] In monastic life, recreation was the scheduled time in the day when the Sisters, otherwise silent in prayer, would come together to speak with one another. Some less formal activities might take place during this time (e.g., viewing photographs or reading letters from other monasteries), but for the most part it was simply a time to gather and socialize. Thus, the article on recreation

concerning recreation and conversation provide a way by which to transform the activity and interactivity of anyone's leisure into a time for living well.

The saint begins with a general principle:

> We ought not think that there is little virtue in recreating properly. We should not, therefore, undertake this time merely out of habit, or as a matter of form, but with preparation and devotion.

As with all the moments of our day, the time we spend in leisure has a decidedly personal purpose; that is, its focus has more to do with the persons involved than with any particular activity. Thus, even leisure beckons us to live virtuously. To do so, St. Francis de Sales invites us to imbue this time with something more than routine habit or simply participating in some activity as a matter of form. Rather, we should approach our free time with the conviction that it can be good for us; if that is the case, then just as we do with all our actions, we should prepare for it and live it with devotion.

As to preparation, once again the first step is a redirecting of our intention:

> When we recreate, we will ask Our Lord for the grace to say and do only what contributes to his glory.

in the original *Spiritual Directory* focuses primarily on spoken interactions.

This initial prayer may be even more necessary during leisure than at work. After all, despite any contingencies or variations, work is usually well defined for us; we know what we have to do, and we address those tasks conscientiously. But leisure is more free and spontaneous, less formal and structured. In this respect, we may not be as conscious of, or vigilant about, speaking and acting appropriately. Hence, the saint reckons it prudent to seek the help of divine grace so that what we say and do will be in accord with the divine will during these times as well.

Concerning those things we do in our leisure time, St. Francis de Sales elsewhere makes abundantly clear that recreational activities are humanly valuable.

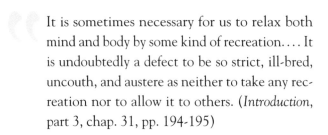

> It is sometimes necessary for us to relax both mind and body by some kind of recreation.... It is undoubtedly a defect to be so strict, ill-bred, uncouth, and austere as neither to take any recreation nor to allow it to others. (*Introduction*, part 3, chap. 31, pp. 194-195)

The recreational activities to which St. Francis refers may be "natural"—such as walking, running, bicycling, hiking, or anything done in the open air. They may also be "skilled"—as in any games or sports that develop our physical or mental capabilities, or both. In either case, doing something is preferred to doing nothing! These activities contribute to our overall well-being and, as such, should be considered valuable means for helping us become who we are.

At the same time, the saint offers the commonsense advice that recreational activities have only a second-order value. That is to say, they are beneficial only inasmuch as they aid us as persons, which they do primarily in terms of providing us with needed relaxation. Beyond that, he cautions us to keep the purpose of the particular activities in mind and to be wary of the personal value we attach to the games we play. As he explains:

> All that is needed is the common prudence that gives due order, time, place and measure to all things.... If we spend too much time on them, they are no longer amusements but tasks in which neither mind nor body is refreshed but rather stupefied and worn out.... If the stakes played for are too high, the players' emotions get out of control. (*Introduction*, part 3, chap. 31, p. 195)[49]

Beyond this activity, a Salesian consideration of leisure takes into greater account our interactivity, in the routine and informal socializing we do. As social beings, we regularly interact with a number of people in a wide variety of settings. These everyday encounters may be merely social or potentially useful or even necessary in virtue of our state in life.[50] And they include what is eminently personal, as in the friendships we form.

[49] As an example of recreation that runs counter to the humanistic purpose of leisure, St. Francis de Sales speaks of gambling ("games of dices, cards, and the like"), to which he objects on the grounds that gambling is founded on luck rather than on reason, tends toward overoccupation of the mind, and leads to profit only at the expense of others (*Introduction*, part 3, chap. 32).

[50] On these distinctions among associations, see *Introduction to the Devout Life*, part 3, chap. 24, pp. 176-179.

Whatever the character of our encounter with others, virtue should abound because those with whom we interact have also been created in the divine image and likeness. Consequently, we would do well to adopt the "rule" that St. Francis de Sales developed as a student at Padua—namely, that he would never disdain or avoid meeting other people.[51] For an emerging young aristocrat, such openness to being sociable was necessary; for a somewhat introverted university student, this posed a great challenge. Yet his practice reveals the twofold relational principle that other people are also children of God and that interacting well with them is essential to our growth and development.

Our approach in relating to others begins with the "look" we bring to our interactions. Although originally written in the context of the closed quarters of a monastery, the exhortation that St. Francis de Sales gives to the Visitation Sisters in the *Spiritual Directory* can be extended to any social setting:

Let us not come to recreation with a sad and disagreeable countenance, but rather with a pleasant and affable one.

Situations impact us in different ways. Our moods will often vary, sometimes to include our being sad and disagreeable. But the psychological space we happen to be in does not need to define the space we occupy with others. Difficult circumstances might make this a challenge, but beginning our encounters with a smile, with a "pleasant and affable" look, always bodes well for

---

[51] See his "Rules for Conversation and Social Gatherings" in the *Spiritual Exercises*, pp. 36-39.

TRUE FRIENDSHIP*

In the Salesian tradition, living well necessarily entails culti-vating right relations not only with God but also with other people. In addition to providing counsels about conversations in the *Introduction to the Devout Life*, St. Francis de Sales writes extensively there about topics dealing with social virtues. Pri-mary among these is the cultivation of true and good friendships.

For St. Francis de Sales, friendship is both necessary and dangerous. Having good friends is necessary, he says, so that we may "encourage, assist, and lead one another to perform good deeds" (*Introduction*, part 3, chap. 19, p. 163). But he also warns that friendship, because it is based on intercommunication, can vary greatly depending on what goods the friends communicate to each other.

On the one hand, false friends exchange empty goods. Re-lationships based on sensual or carnal pleasures are contrary to who we are as spiritual persons and have "no more right to the title of friendship among [people] than that of asses and horses for like effects" (*Introduction*, part 3, chap. 17, p. 158). So, too, friendships that follow from frivolous amusements or deceitful intentions are vain and foolish and potentially evil.

On the other hand, true friends exchange what is good for both persons, such as knowledge, virtue, charity, and devotion. Friendships like this, the saint says, are few in number but pre-cious in value. "It will be excellent because it comes from God,

---

* See *Introduction to the Devout Life*, part 3, chaps. 17-22, pp. 157-171.

excellent because it leads to God, excellent because its bond will endure eternally in God. How good it is," he exclaims, "to love here on earth as they love in heaven and to learn to cherish one another in this world as we shall do eternally in the next!" (*Introduction*, part 3, chap. 19, pp. 162-163). Certainly, St. Francis's deeply personal and profoundly spiritual friendship with Jane de Chantal embodies this saintly vision.

With the odd yet true image that "our heart breathes through the ear" (*Introduction*, part 3, chap. 21, p. 167), St. Francis de Sales reminds us that how and what we communicate with those we call our friends is a key to living well.

the interaction that follows.[52] And when it comes to those verbal interactions, the saint offers several insights that champion respect for the one who is speaking, the one who is listening, and the subject matter of their conversation.

St. Francis de Sales bases his advice about conversations on the sound conviction that speech reveals something about the speaker, for "our words are a true indication of the state of our souls" (*Introduction*, part 3, chap. 26, p. 181). With this principle

---

[52] Similarly, the attire with which we appear before others has an effect on our interactions. For this reason, St. Francis de Sales also counsels decency in dress: "It is a sort of contempt of those you associate with to frequent their company in unbecoming attire.... I would have devout people, whether men or women, always [be] the best dressed in a group but the least pompous and affected" (*Introduction*, part 3, chap. 25, p. 180).

in mind, he writes a word of encouragement as well as a word of caution in the *Spiritual Directory*:

> Just as we should converse in a spirit of simplicity and openness, so, too, should we take pleasure in speaking often of good and holy topics.
>
> If we be inclined to speak too much about ourselves or are subject to other faults like this, let us, in beginning a conversation, briefly recall this imperfection and resolve to be on guard against it. To this end, we should implore the grace of the Holy Spirit and the help of our guardian angel.

Although everyday situations might not often present opportunities for speaking about God or "holy topics" directly, when an occasion does arise, we should welcome the chance to indicate our concern for living devoutly. Yet, as St. Francis reminds us, we should do so with humility and docility: "Always speak of God as God, that is, reverently and devoutly, not with outward show or affectation but in a spirit of meekness, charity, and humility.... Never speak of God or devotion in a routine or thoughtless manner, but always with attention and reverence" (*Introduction*, part 3, chap. 26, pp. 181, 182). Conversely, the natural tendency to speak about ourselves remains something to be wary of and, out of respect for others, to curtail as best we can with divine assistance.

The flip side of this modesty shows itself as a respect for the person with whom we converse. To put this into practice, St. Francis de Sales warns us about three common tendencies in leisurely conversations — indecency, immodesty, and impudence:

Be careful never to let an indecent word leave your lips, for even if you do not speak with an evil intention, those who hear it may take it in a different way. (*Introduction*, part 3, chap. 27, p. 182)

When immodest words are subtly and hypocritically concealed they become more poisonous. (*Introduction*, part 3, chap. 27, pp. 182-183)

Nothing is so opposed to charity, and much more to devotion, than to despise and condemn one's neighbor. (*Introduction*, part 3, chap. 27, p. 183)

Modifying these imperfections in our speech enables us to engage others more charitably and thus "to pass our recreation time in such a way that we may gain a holy eternity by devotion" (*Introduction*, part 3, chap. 27, p. 184).

Finally, with regard to the topics of discussion, St. Francis de Sales also offers advice to counter problematic conversations and to promote beneficial interactions.

On the one hand, he cautions against rash judgment (*Introduction*, part 3, chap. 28, pp. 184-188). This happens when we draw a conclusion from someone's action in order to condemn that person. It is rash inasmuch as our passing judgment usurps the role of God as sole judge of us and because we have enough to judge ourselves on without rushing to pass judgment on others. To remedy this all-too-common way of speaking about those not present, the saint suggests an alternative approach:

If an action has many different aspects, we must always think of which is the best.... [But] when a just man can no longer explain either the fact or the intention of someone whom he otherwise knows to be virtuous, he still will not pass judgment on him but puts it out of his mind and leaves the judgment to God.... When we cannot excuse a sin, let us at least make it worthy of compassion by attributing the most favorable cause we can to it, such as ignorance or weakness. (*Introduction*, part 3, chap. 28, pp. 186, 187)

Our tendency to speak rashly about others runs the risk of going to the extreme of slander. St. Francis de Sales, himself the object of such speech, considers this "the true plague of society" because "of all external goods a good name is the best." Slander reveals its ugly self when those conversing give in to

falsely imputing crimes and sins to your neighbor, revealing his secret sins, exaggerating those that are manifest, putting an evil interpretation on his good works, denying the good that you know belongs to someone, [or] maliciously concealing it or lessening it by words. (*Introduction*, part 3, chap. 29, p. 189)

To counteract this vice, which often appears hidden behind humor or sarcasm, the saint counsels a multifaceted exercise by which we can spare the person being maligned:

When you hear anyone spoken ill of, make the accusation doubtful if you can do so justly. If you cannot, excuse the intention of the accused party. If that cannot be done, express sympathy for him, change the subject of conversation, remembering yourself and causing the rest to recall that those who do not fall into sin owe it all to God's grace. Recall the slanderer to himself in a mild way and tell of some good deed of the offended party if you know of any. (*Introduction*, part 3, chap. 27, pp. 192-193)

Ultimately, we divinize our leisurely conversation by exercising three virtues that in the Salesian tradition are central to a devout life, and St. Francis de Sales explains these in no uncertain terms. First, our conversations should be honest and based always on *truth*:

> Be on guard against equivocation, ambiguity, or dissimulation. While it is not always advisable to say all that is true, it is never permissible to speak against the truth.... An honest explanation always has more grace and force to excuse us than a lie has. (*Introduction*, part 3, chap. 30, p. 193)

Similarly, whenever we speak we should do so with *simplicity*, saying what we mean and meaning what we say, so that our listeners will not have to read between the lines of our speech to figure out what is really intended:

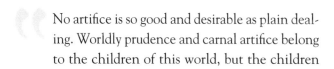

> No artifice is so good and desirable as plain dealing. Worldly prudence and carnal artifice belong to the children of this world, but the children

of God walk a straight path and their heart is
without guile.... Lying, double-dealing, and
dissimulation are always signs of a weak, mean
mind. (*Introduction*, part 3, chap. 30, p. 193)

Finally, when we speak, we should always remember to be *gentle*
because words do have power:

> Nothing is ever gained by harshness. To speak
> little ... does not consist in uttering only a few
> words but in uttering none that are useless.
> With regard to speech, we must not look to the
> quantity but rather to the quality of our words.
> (*Introduction*, part 3, chap. 30, p. 194)

What St. Francis de Sales advises in terms of speech obviously
refers to in-person conversations. These days, we can extend his
advice to the interactivity facilitated by digital media. While
online encounters take place virtually, they are nevertheless real
interactions between real people. Whether posting images or
messages, this form of recreation and conversation should likewise avoid vice and exemplify virtue. The media may be new,
but Salesian wisdom offers a practical way to invest all social
communications with a measure of devotion that renders this
contemporary form of leisure as a way to live well today.

9

THE EXAMEN:
REVIEWING OUR
DAILY PROGRESS

By proposing a prayerful way to conduct the activities of daily life common to everyone (from awakening to eating and working and relaxing), the *Spiritual Directory* encompasses the vast majority of a typical day and offers a roadmap for spiritual growth throughout the day. Now, before the final act of going to sleep at night, St. Francis de Sales recommends that we take a few moments to consider how we have progressed along the way.

Actually, the saint suggests that we make an examination of conscience at several times during the day, but the primary exercise takes place in the evening (or, more practically, at night, before retiring to bed). The goal of this examen is simply to gauge our growth today so as to become aware of those things on which we need to improve tomorrow. In this way, the popular aphorisms of classical humanism (such as "know thyself" and "the unexamined life is not worth living") encounter the humility of Salesian spirituality, to yield nothing else than the honest recognition of all aspects of our life—both positive (graces) and negative (faults)—before God, who is the source of our existence.

> In the evening, we will thank Our Lord for all his benefits, especially for the grace of our vocation and for having willed to preserve us during the day, providing for all our needs through this sweet goodness.

The examen begins, just as the day did, with an act of thanksgiving. Having lived through the gift of one more day's existence, we recognize our Lord as giver and sustainer of that gift. Along with our vocation, or state in life, we also give thanks for all that took place during the day as an expression of divine providence on our behalf. Through this "lively consideration of graces received," we come to realize the truth "that none of the good in us comes from ourselves" (*Introduction*, part 3, chap. 5, p. 124). In turn, this recognition of goodness inspires a sense of thankfulness that we can foster each day, something that scientific research demonstrates as having positive psychological benefits as well.

But, of course, there is more.

> We must confess and acknowledge before God that the day has not passed without our having offended him in some way.

Why we must confess our faults is simple: no one is perfect! In relation to the divine perfection, we fail every day in some way, however small or great. As each of us knows from experience, temptations abound in every realm of life, and there is always room for improvement. To make that improvement, however, we first need to acknowledge where we need to grow.

Sometimes, though, the temptations win. And no one likes to admit failure. Thus:

> Because everyone is blind in his own concerns, we should ask for the grace and the light of the Holy Spirit to know our faults clearly.

Shining a spiritual light on ourselves, we will see how we rationalize our shortcomings so as to give a more positive spin to the way we live; in this, we turn a blind eye to the truth about ourselves that should be our real concern. Knowing this pervasive human tendency, St. Francis de Sales again recommends, as he does for all our daily actions, that at the beginning of our examination of conscience we first ask for grace so that we can come to know ourselves better by knowing our faults clearly.

> Then we will begin by reviewing our actions, words and thoughts since our last examination of conscience. Reciting some penitential formula, we will humbly ask Our Lord pardon for our faults.

Self-improvement begins with self-knowledge. Who we are, in relation to God, comes to be revealed in the choices we make each day and is expressed in the deeds that follow those decisions. Conversely, the choices we make also shape us into the persons we are continually becoming. The examination of conscience simply reviews this cyclical reality of being human.

FACING TEMPTATIONS

Notwithstanding his optimism, St. Francis de Sales recognizes the struggles we face and in part 4 of his *Introduction to the Devout Life* offers advice on what to do in the face of temptations. To begin, he distinguishes between pleasure and consent, the former being natural and the latter being a matter of our choice: "Never think yourself overcome as long as [temptations] are displeasing to you," for "our soul does not always have power not to feel the temptation, but it can always refuse to consent to it" (*Introduction*, part 4, chap. 3, p. 227).

He then offers very practical advice: when dealing with great temptations, we should implore God's help, turn our thoughts to what is good, and remain steadfast in our refusal to consent. Concerning smaller temptations, "it is impossible to be completely free from being plagued by them" and therefore "our best defense is not to disturb ourselves too much over them" (*Introduction*, part 4, chap. 9, p. 236). He eschews any sense of interior debate or dispute with the temptations in favor of simply and gently dismissing them.

Especially dangerous are temptations to anxiety or sadness (which Francis de Sales knows well from his personal experience as a student in Paris). He claims that "with the single exception of sin, anxiety is the greatest evil that can happen to a soul." Due to its power, the saint advises that we treat ourselves gently in that state: "you must be especially careful both to put your mind at rest and in peace and to have a calm judgment and will. Then try gently and meekly to accomplish your desire, taking in regular order the most convenient means" (*Introduction*, part 4, chap. 11, p. 239). He describes sadness as that which "disturbs and upsets the soul, arouses inordinate fears … stupefies and oppresses the brain … and destroys [the mind's] strength" (*Introduction*, part 4, chap. 12, p. 241). To overcome this sorry state, he encourages prayer to God, who alone is our joy and consolation, perseverance in vigorous opposition to any tendency to sadness, doing good works even if they bring no immediate comfort, and resigning ourselves to God's hands with the faith that "after God has put you on trial he will deliver you from this evil" (*Introduction*, part 4, chap. 12, p. 243).

So, at the conclusion of each day, we review our *actions* in terms of their conformity with the divine will for us. What did we do (or not do) this day to obey God's signified will for us? How well did we accept God's good pleasure in our lives this day?

But St. Francis de Sales invites us to a deeper spiritual consciousness by having us also examine our words. In the *Introduction to the Devout Life*, he makes the connection between our spiritual well-being and our speech: "Physicians learn about a [person's] health or sickness by looking at his tongue and our words are a true indication of the state of our souls" (*Introduction*, part 3, chap. 26, 181). Have our words this day conveyed truth? Have we spoken them with charity?

Behind our words lie our thoughts. Even if not expressed vocally, our thoughts can shape the way we see ourselves, others, and the world around us. This is especially true of thoughts that we purposely dwell on, which gives them power to grow and to influence what we say and do. What has been on our minds this day? What has fueled our imagination and consideration? Did we think good or kind thoughts and cut short any bad or uncharitable ones?

Ultimately, the key to this examination of conscience is not so much to make a detailed moral analysis of the content of our actions, words, and thoughts. Rather, the Salesian emphasis remains on the person in relation to God. How has what we did or said or thought this day been a response to God's ever-present grace and inspiration? How have those thoughts and words and deeds contributed to, or detracted from, the good life we are called to live? And, most importantly, how might we grow and improve in those areas tomorrow?

With this general schema in mind, St. Francis de Sales offers further advice on how to practice this spiritual exercise:

> To make this examination easier, it will be helpful for us when we commit some fault during the day to examine ourselves right away, consider briefly our motive, humble ourselves before God and make a mental note of this fault in order to include it in the examination that evening.

Here he counsels a more immediate examination of conscience. In keeping with his emphasis on the present moment, he seeks to capture that moment when we know that we have committed some fault or failed in some way. To examine this action right away gives us the best possibility of clearly understanding what we have done (or not done). Here we see again that the holy Doctor focuses our attention less on the actions than on our self-awareness and on our relation to God. Self-awareness comes with an appreciation of our motives at the time, while our relation to God calls for a continual recognition of our imperfections before the Almighty (humility).

And, in typically practical Salesian terms, examining our deeds "in the moment" will make it easier to do so in the evening before retiring.

> In addition to this examination common to all, we may make a particular one. This concerns the practice of a special virtue most useful to us and directly opposed to those imperfections toward which we feel ourselves more inclined.

Consistent with his humanistic focus on self-development aided by grace, St. Francis de Sales here suggests the practice of a *particular* examen. Assuming that we have identified for ourselves a goal, or an area of life in which to improve, this examination considers our daily progress in that specific realm. And in keeping with his understanding of devotion as something particular to each person's state in life, St. Francis refers here to "the practice of a special virtue." Perhaps we need to grow in patience or humility or gentleness or any of the other little virtues (to be explained in chapter 12). By seeking ways to practice a particular virtue throughout the day, we can counteract those imperfections toward which prior examinations have revealed we may be inclined.

The particular examen with regard to virtue discloses St. Francis de Sales's optimistic pedagogy. How we can get better at doing good is a much more inspiring approach than dwelling on our faults and failings! Still, the fact remains that we are not flawless, in either our actions or our understanding.

> If in our examination we find no faults, let us humble ourselves profoundly before God and thank him, admitting nevertheless that we have committed some faults about which we have neither recollection nor awareness.

Even, or especially, in our imperfect and sinful state, the saint counsels us to give thanks to God, for it is divine grace that sustains us in every moment and God's redeeming mercy that is offered to us each day.

But the various forms of the examination of conscience are not merely exercises in personal awareness. The ultimate purpose of this spiritual practice is to aid in the transformation (and conversion) of our lives. Thus, St. Francis de Sales advises us to conclude the examination with these acts:

> We will make a firm resolution to correct ourselves with the help of God's grace, which we should request with all the love and devotion within our power.

In the Salesian tradition, the act of praying should have practical results; that is to say, our prayer should have a concrete effect on how we live.[53] By making a "firm resolution" to change

---

[53] In his methodology for mental prayer (further explained in chapter 11), St. Francis de Sales recognizes that "meditation produces

the ways we have come to see in our examinations, aided by God's grace, we are more likely to grow and improve and less likely to see the same faults and failings repeated, although that might happen — in which case, we repeat the process yet again, but always humbly and gently.

> After this, we will recommend our soul, our body, our whole being to the mercy of God. We will pray for the Church, our parents and relatives, and all those toward whom we have a special obligation; we ought not [to] forget the poor souls in purgatory. We should greet our Lady, our guardian angel and holy patrons.

The examination of conscience is a decidedly personal exercise and demands honest introspection. But it also calls forth a recognition of others. First and foremost, it affirms, with gratitude, the power of God's mercy, which so far surpasses our actions that we do well to commend ourselves, in the entirety of our being, to that divine power. But the examen also brings us into communion with others, fellow sinners who can benefit from our prayers: those in the community of the Church on earth, those who have a significant place in our lives, and those who have gone before us in death, especially the poor souls in purgatory. By also greeting the saints, we end our examination with the reminder that sharing their eternal life is also our ultimate vocation, and the reason we seek to live each day well.

---

devout movements in the will, the affective part of our soul." But he adds that one should not dwell only there but instead change the affections into resolutions "for your own correction and improvement" (*Introduction*, part 2, chap. 6, p. 78).

10

ON RETIRING:
PRACTICING DETACHMENT

Finally the day is done. Our work is over and our conversations concluded, at least for now. We have had the opportunity to examine our progress in living the good life and have identified where we might do better tomorrow. Now bedtime beckons and, we hope, a good night's sleep.

For St. Francis de Sales, even this seemingly inconsequential time presents an opportunity for spiritual growth. In the context of his everyday spirituality, and as a bookend to the article on rising, going to bed at night represents the final opportunity to live the day well. Our experiences of sleep might vary greatly — from dozing off as soon as our head hits the pillow, to tossing and turning, to staring blankly at the ceiling, unable to go to sleep or go back to sleep once awakened. But more than offering bodily rejuvenation, retiring to bed presents us with a way to practice abandonment to the divine goodness of God's providence.

This spiritual exercise begins even before we get under the covers:

> While undressing, we should keep our mind attentive as much as possible to spiritual matters.

For the Sisters of the Visitation, bedtime came rather early, and their saintly founder counsels them to begin attuning their thoughts to the next day's early morning meditation. By contrast, the hour for sleep for most of us probably comes as a welcome relief after a long day's grind. It tends to be less an intentional activity than a capitulation to exhaustion, a semiconscious collapse that begins as soon as the late-night television show is turned off. For this reason, St. Francis de Sales speaks of the need to be *attentive* — to engage in conscious thinking about things that matter in a way that would otherwise not happen naturally. As with all progress in the good life, this, too, takes some effort, especially at the end of the day, after our minds have been focused on so many other matters. To facilitate this spiritual attentiveness, St. Francis suggests that we associate it with the nightly routine of undressing (just as he also suggested for getting dressed in the morning). In this way, the spiritual merges more easily with the material, and we learn to divinize even this ordinary deed.

To assist us further with being attentive to spiritual matters, and to keep us in the present so we do not begin planning ahead or worrying about tomorrow, the saint offers two vivid images for us to consider:

> In bed we ought to remember that Our Lord and some saints used to sleep on the cold ground, and how much we are obliged to love and serve him, since his gentle goodness provides for our slightest

comforts in such a fatherly way. Lying there, we should picture to ourselves that one day we will be like this in the grave and ask God to assist us at the hour of death. Let us act as if we were seeing Our Lord with our own eyes, for he really sees us in this action as well as in any other.

The first image — that of sleeping on the cold ground — may appeal to campers, but it contrasts with the more typical experience of collapsing into a comfortable bed. No matter its shape or size, having a bed to sleep in — along with a roof over our heads — is yet another of the daily gifts we enjoy (while so many others in the world do not). Recognizing this gift, like others, as coming ultimately from divine providence and the fatherly hand of God attunes us to the source of all goodness. In gratitude, therefore, we also recognize our creaturely obligation to respond with lives of love for our families and service to our neighbors.

The second image may be less appealing, but it is no less spiritually motivating. As we considered in the article on work, an imaginative consideration of our mortality is not intended to be morbid. Rather, it confronts an existential reality with a spiritual vision. One day death will happen. To prepare ourselves for that eventuality, with prayers for divine assistance now and at that hour, is to see that even in the direst of times — such as our lying in a grave — that same providential and fatherly God is with us. And therein lies our greatest comfort. Detached spiritually from the things of this world, as we will be materially at the time of death, we can entrust ourselves into God's hands now, before that mortal moment. And we do this confidently by using the eyes of our mind to develop a vivid consciousness of seeing our

Lord, not in a dream but as if he were really looking upon and seeing us—as, in fact, he does.

With a spiritual attentiveness that seeks to conclude the day in the same way that it began, St. Francis de Sales suggests:

> We should always try to fall asleep with some good thought.

Just as we can bring about a more positive day by beginning with a good thought (explained in chapter 3), so we can increase our chances of getting some rest by ending the day with the thought of something good or holy.

Still, we know that does not always work! Some nights are restless. Even saints suffer from these sleepless nights, as it seems St. Francis de Sales did. But in his experiential wisdom, he counsels us even then to make use of the situation to turn to God through the power of spiritual aspirations:

> If we awaken during the night, we will stir up our heart immediately with these words:
>
> *At midnight someone shouted: The groom is here! Come out and greet him.* (Matt. 25:6)

Drawing from the inspirations of Sacred Scripture, St. Francis de Sales encourages us to transform undesired restlessness into purposeful attentiveness, to change our interrupted slumber into directed thought. In particular, the darkness of our surroundings creates a context for this spiritual consciousness:

SALESIAN INDIFFERENCE

For St. Francis de Sales, the simple act of going to sleep represents, in miniature, the exercise of spiritual detachment or abandonment that should characterize the conversion of our entire life. Psychologically, going to sleep invites us to let go of the cares and concerns of the day in order to get some rest. Spiritually, it calls us to let go of our dreams and desires, in the faith-based recognition that God's care for us is greater than anything we seek in this life.

In Salesian spirituality this letting go leads to growth in the spiritual virtue of "indifference." Far from the usual meaning of that word in terms of not being interested or not caring, St. Francis de Sales speaks of indifference as the crowning achievement of the spiritual life. In the last of his *Spiritual Conferences* to the Sisters of the Visitation,* the founder offers a final farewell to them. In response to one last question, he says:

> Do you ask what I desire should remain most deeply engraved upon your mind, so that you may put it in practice? Ah, my dear daughters, what shall I say, except those excellent words I have so often already recommended to you: Desire nothing, refuse nothing. These words say everything, for they teach us the practice of perfect indifference. (p. 405)

* St. Francis de Sales, *Spiritual Conferences* (Library of St. Francis de Sales), trans. Francis A Gasquet and Henry B. Mackey (London: Burns and Oates, 1909), pp. 399-406.

The words "already recommended," as well as the theological basis for them, are found earlier in that same conference, when he teaches them "that we must neither ask anything nor refuse anything, but leave ourselves absolutely in the arms of divine Providence, without busying ourselves with any desires, except to will what God wills of us" (p. 400).

In his *Treatise on the Love of God*, St. Francis offers the poignant image of a statue in a niche to illustrate his conviction: "if we love [God] we sleep not only in his sight, but at his pleasure, and not only by his will, but also according to his will.... Then at our waking, if we reflect upon it, we find that God was ever present with us, and that we were in no wise absent or separated from him" (*Treatise*, book 6, chap. 11, p. 264). In this way, a holy indifference, more so than frenzied activity, leads to peace—at night and throughout life.

From the view of the darkness around us, we will turn to a consideration of the darkness of our own soul and of all sinners and offer this prayer:

O Lord, since your merciful heart made you come down from heaven to earth to visit us, please enlighten those who lie prostrate in the darkness of ignorance and in the shadow of eternal death; if it be your will, guide them also into the path of interior peace. (Luke 1:78-79)

PRACTICING DETACHMENT

From the exterior night he bids us move to consider the interior darkness, which in our soul results from the effects of sin. Aware of the existential reality of our ignorance and imperfection, we pray to be enlightened by the Good News of the Incarnation, when the eternal Light came into this world with the offer of the gift of peace.

At times we will turn to our God, our Savior, and say:

You neither slumber nor sleep, you who guard the Israel of our souls. (Ps. 121:7)

The most intense darkness of midnight can present no obstacle to your divine activity; at that hour you were born of the holy virgin, your Mother; at that hour, too, you can cause your heavenly graces to be born in our souls and completely fill us with your choicest blessings. Merciful Redeemer, so enlighten my poor blind heart with the beautiful rays of your grace that it may never remain in any way in the death of sin; oh, I beg you, do not allow my invisible enemies to say:

We have overcome him. (Ps. 13:4)

Theological thinking does not happen easily during the day, let alone in the fitful hours of late night or early morning. But if we can attune our senses at these times to the meaningfulness of God's manifestations at similar times — his birth and death and Resurrection — we open ourselves to the experience of divine grace and the power to overcome our deepest fears.

Still, we would also like to get back to sleep! Even that desire can have a spiritual dimension:

> Finally, after having considered the darkness and the imperfections of our soul, we may say with Isaiah:
>
> *Watchman, watchman, does much of the night of our imperfections still remain? (21:11-12)*
>
> And we will hear him answer us:
>
> *The morning of good inspirations has come; why do you love the darkness more than the light? (John 3:19)*

We hope that this prayerful dialogue will not keep us awake longer but will instead give us the peace to fall asleep again. Should it not, more holy words are suggested:

> In addition, we may use these holy words:
>
> *Neither the sun nor its rays are my principal light, but God alone, who is as merciful to me by night as he is by day.*

Whatever the cause of his intermittent insomnia and his apparent fear of the dark, St. Francis de Sales recognizes that even these all-too-human realities hold the potential for contributing to a good life. Although he proposes several specific thoughts to consider during the night, recalling the specific biblical quotes is not necessary (and hardly possible without practice). Instead, his pedagogical point is to have us extend into the night the spiritual precept of calling to mind God's presence and being attentive to God's will throughout the day. Whatever form it takes in the thoughts we muster, that spiritual consciousness is the foundation to leading a good life—and also to getting a good night's sleep!

PART 3

SACRED MOMENTS

A Salesian approach to the good life—an everyday strategy for personal growth and development—seeks to create a daily routine by which we become ever more focused on, and responsive to, the presence of God in the ordinary events of a single day. By paying attention to divine grace, and directing the intention of our actions to be in accord with that grace, we transform our tasks and responsibilities into opportunities for living each day well.

But leading the good life entails more than simply managing our daily routines with a view toward growing in holiness. It also means dedicating ourselves to particular actions that give greater prominence to the religious character of our lives.

In the Salesian tradition, we can identify such sacred moments in the time for prayer, the practice of virtue, and the celebration of sacraments. These specifically religious activities make it possible to encounter God in a more direct way, which St. Francis de Sales describes to the Visitation Sisters by using a classic image. "The Sacraments," he says, "are channels through which, so to speak, God descends to us, as we through prayer ascend to Him, since prayer is nothing else than the lifting up of our mind and heart to God" (*Spiritual Conferences*, p. 347).

This channeling of divine grace, in turn, enables us to elevate our lives to a greater good. How this works we shall explore in this last part of our guide, which comments on the Salesian method of meditation, the cultivation of "little virtues," the sacrament of Reconciliation, and active participation in the Mass.

11

PRAYER:
COMMUNING WITH
THE DIVINE

Although it treats of religious customs and practices in the life of a monastery, St. Francis de Sales's *Spiritual Directory* surprisingly does not include specific instructions on how to pray in a formal way. The saint's only advice to the Sisters in this regard is that they consult "other good books" in harmony with those that he himself wrote. And he encourages them in this, as in all things, to "heed the inspiration of the Holy Spirit and the direction given them" by this divine guide.

Nevertheless, in the *Spiritual Directory* he does affirm the central importance of prayer. Since the intention and objective of living well is to be united with God, prayerful communication with God is essential.

But the question remains: how can we pray, especially when our harried lives are filled with other time-consuming tasks and responsibilities? As we have seen in part 2, one way to be prayerful is to transform the activities of our state in life into actions done for and with the love of God. Another way, equally necessary, is to dedicate some time to conversing directly with God—that is, to pray.

When we consider what prayer is, we tend to think of it as speaking to God in holy words. This manner of vocal prayer includes traditional words we recite from memory (e.g., the Lord's Prayer and the Hail Mary), intercessory words by which we petition for divine help, and ritual words we speak as part of a liturgical celebration. As necessary and valuable as these are, St. Francis de Sales also recommends another form of prayer for those seeking to lead a good life, a mental rather than vocal prayer that typically goes by the name of meditation or contemplation.[54] Although that sounds like something specific to the life of monks and nuns, the method of praying that the saint offers in the second part of his *Introduction to the Devout Life* is something that anyone can practice.

Meditation in the Salesian tradition is a prayer of the mind and heart. It follows the example of Jesus, who at important moments in his public ministry would often go off by himself to a quiet place to pray and thus to be in communion with the Father and the Spirit. The saint makes use of a familiar image to depict the pedagogical power of prayer: "just as little children learn to speak by listening to their mothers and lisping words with them, so also by keeping close to our Savior in meditation

[54] See book 6 of his *Treatise*, where, in chapter 2, he distinguishes meditation from thought (the musings of the mind) and from study (whose goal is to learn). He then explains (in chapters 3 through 5) how meditation differs from contemplation inasmuch as the former is a consideration of the divine mystery undertaken in a somewhat painstaking and detailed manner, while the latter is a more collective view of the divine that requires no labor to behold.

and observing his words, actions, and affections we learn by his grace to speak, act, and will like him" (*Introduction*, part 2, chap. 1, p. 71). Salesian meditation provides the way to keep close to the Savior. Conceived as a form of inspired imagining, it focuses more on listening to God than on speaking to God (as we do in vocal prayers). Through this prayerful attentiveness, we grow in understanding and increase our motivation to lead a good life.

Because meditating is not a common practice for people caught up in the hectic pace of ordinary life, St. Francis de Sales offers a method that can be adapted to any lifestyle and adopted by everyone. Still, as he is wont to say, the method is not the key; following the inspiration of the Spirit remains paramount in prayer.

The Salesian method for meditation begins with an intentional preparation. Practically speaking, talking to someone who is not physically present with us poses a great challenge, to say the least (though social media has rendered this much easier nowadays). The ancient dictum "out of sight, out of mind" rings true here. Because we do not see God, it seems odd, if not impossible, actually to converse with God. For this reason, the saint counsels us first to draw our minds briefly to a consideration of God's never-ending presence with us. Because God's presence is not immediate or obvious, we must intentionally make the effort to be cognizant of it. This cognition, in turn, more easily evokes a sense of prayerful reverence.

PRESENCE

To become aware of God's presence, the saint suggests four means, any one of which will ready us for mental prayer (*Introduction*, part 2, chap. 2).

1. *Recall that God is everywhere.* "The first consists of a lively, attentive realization of God's absolute presence, that is, that God is in all things and all places" (p. 73). This is a basic tenet of religious belief. God is. Being eternal, God always is. Being transcendental, God is everywhere. As Creator, God is implicated in all that is. We know these truths intellectually, and we affirm them as a matter of faith. But, as the saint wisely notes, "Although faith assures us of his presence, yet because we do not see him with our eyes we often forget about him and behave as if God were far distant from us" (p. 74). So, if we wish to pray well, to speak with and listen to God, a first preparation consists in making ourselves aware that God is.

2. *Recall that God is present within us.* A second means of being aware of God's presence is "to remember that he is not only in the place where [we] are but also that he is present in a most particular manner in [our] heart and in the very center of [our] spirit" (p. 74). As the giver and sustainer of all life, God is present to us in the very act of our existing as living beings. Consider, for a moment, that we breathe. This is not something we choose to do, as we choose other actions, yet it is also something we cannot help but do (no matter how long we might be able to hold our breath!). With this realization, we see that something (or Someone) else is at work within us, animating us and enabling us to be alive. That something is breath, which in the ancient religious languages is the same word as "spirit." That Someone is God.

3. *Consider Christ's gaze from heaven.* A third way of realizing God's presence in our lives is "to consider how

our Savior in his humanity gazes down from heaven" on all human beings (p. 74). Admittedly, this is more imaginative than actual, but it is no less real. Watch what happens when people speak of God or think of heaven: almost naturally they look up! The vastness and majesty of space above us leads to the thought of One looking down upon us.

4. *Picture Christ near you.* Finally, the fourth way St. Francis de Sales suggests for being attentive to God's presence consists in "represent[ing] to ourselves the Savior in his sacred humanity as if he were near us, just as we sometimes imagine a friend to be" (p. 75). This mental picture underscores the reality of God's presence with the image of someone walking beside us and talking to us. At one time, God actually did this, in the person of Jesus. Now that presence is no longer physical, but through faith God remains similarly close by.

Having prepared ourselves to pray by calling to mind the real and close presence of God in our lives, we then proceed to invoke God's help. This is simply calling upon God (even silently) in the confident hope that God will speak to us.

IMAGINATION

Then comes the specifically "mental" step. St. Francis de Sales, like other spiritual guides, bids us to turn our attention to a particular mystery of God. By this he means that we use our imagination to focus on a particular place or action or scene in which God acts. This is most easily accomplished by carefully reading a biblical story and picturing ourselves as being present in it. By focusing our minds in this way, we insert ourselves into the story. We see what is happening. We hear the words being spoken. We touch those present. By means of our physical senses, we conjure the reality of the divine mystery before us. It may seem like making things up, but focusing our attention in this way really serves to re-present the event to us and thus to draw us into an encounter with God.

CONSIDERATION

With that mystery in mind, we then allow the Spirit to guide us from thought to feeling to action. By an act of the mind, we give consideration to one or more thoughts about the scene we are picturing. What is going on there? What do we see and hear? What do we think—about the event, about God's speaking or acting there, or both, and about ourselves as reliving that event?

AFFECTION

These or similar considerations are intended to excite in us a sense of the holy, an affection in our hearts that inspires us in a sacred way. St. Francis de Sales enumerates the possible feelings we may have as a result of these considerations:

> love of God and neighbor, desire for heaven and glory, zeal for the salvation of souls, imitation of the life of our Lord, compassion, awe, joy, fear of God's displeasure, judgment, and hell, hatred of sin, confidence in God's goodness and mercy, and deep sorrow for the sins of our past life. (*Introduction*, part 2, chap. 6, p. 78)

RESOLUTION

Whatever the type of affection we might experience, the point here is to allow our hearts to be moved by divine inspiration. And being so stirred to feel something from God and for God, we will thereby be moved to act in accord with the divine will.

And this last step is essential. Devotion, according to St. Francis de Sales, is not simply a thought or a feeling. The good life is one that is lived! Thus, Salesian mental prayer always includes a resolution, a decision to act in a specific way in the present moment of this day that aligns our human reality with the divine mystery about which we have prayed.

Presence, imagination, consideration, affection, and reso-lution — these are the elements of meditation in the Salesian tradition. With some practice, the exercise of meditation will flow more seamlessly than the explanation given here. To see how this might work, consider the following example from the Gospel story of the Transfiguration (Mark 9:2-10).

First, place yourself on the mountaintop, in the presence of Jesus along with Peter, James, and John. Consider what you see there. What does Jesus' sudden transformation into a dazzlingly white figure provoke in you? Consider the appearance of Elijah and Moses. In the presence of such dramatic historical figures, how would you react? Listen to the voice that speaks of the beloved Son. What is he saying to you at this moment? Let the affections stir within. Realize that, like the apostles, you are being invited to partake of something supernatural. Recognize that this transformation is what awaits the one who believes in God. Perhaps the experience is fearful, considering how unwor-thy you are to be in the presence of such holiness. Perhaps the experience is awesome, in the supernatural grandeur on display before you. Then, moved by these affections (or others), ponder what you can do this day as a response to your experience of the divine. Peter thought of building three tents, but that was not to be. What can or should you do? Resolve to put that idea into practice as a way to "listen to him," as the heavenly voice on the mountaintop entreats us.

Praying in this meditative way takes time, but even if done quickly, or less deliberately than is outlined in these steps, each part of the process is, in itself, an act of prayer. No matter how much time we can devote to this spiritual exercise, the key is to stir the affections and carry out the resolutions. In this way, we will reap the benefits of prayer throughout the day.

To weave the grace of meditation into the fabric of our lives, or even to supply for it on those days when other responsibilities preclude having sufficient time for mental prayer, St. Francis de Sales offers two related counsels.

The first implores us to gather a "spiritual bouquet" from our prayer, which he describes in this way:

> People who have been walking about in a beautiful garden do not like to leave without gathering in their hands four or five flowers to smell and keep for the rest of the day. In the same way, when our soul has carefully considered by meditation a certain mystery, we should select one, two, or three points that we liked best and that are most adapted to our improvement, think frequently about them, and smell them spiritually during the rest of the day. (*Introduction*, part 2, chap. 7, p. 79)

LIBERTY OF SPIRIT

As in all things spiritual, St. Francis de Sales prizes the freedom that communing with God brings about. In a letter to Jane de Chantal, he explains this in relation to the prayer that Jesus taught his disciples:

> We pray to God above all, that His name may be hallowed, that His kingdom come, that His will be done on earth as it is in heaven. All this is nothing other than the spirit of freedom; for, provided that the name of God is hallowed, that His kingdom is coming in us, that His will is being done, a free spirit has no other concern. (*Letters of Spiritual Direction*, p. 138)

This liberty of spirit, developed through meditation, yields positive benefits for our other activities, including a sense of inner peace and the development of a gentle disposition that enables us to act charitably toward the wants and needs of others.

This spiritual freedom also helps us face the challenge of balancing time devoted to God in prayer and the time needed to complete the many tasks of our state in life. In the same letter, the saint gives the example of someone whose meditation is interrupted by having something else to do:

> A person who has this true freedom will leave her prayer, unruffled, gracious toward the person

who has unexpectedly disturbed her, for to her it's all the same — serving God by meditating or serving Him by responding to her neighbor. Both are the will of God, but helping the neighbor is necessary at that particular moment. We have occasion to practice this freedom whenever things don't go the way we'd like them to; for anyone who is not attached to her own ways will not get impatient when things go otherwise. (*Letters of Spiritual Direction*, pp. 138-139)

St. Francis de Sales was a shining example of this prayerful freedom amid the duties of daily life. In a letter, St. Jane wrote this about him:

For several years before he died he was hardly able to set aside any time for prayer because he was overwhelmed by work; and one day when I asked him whether he had prayed, he said: "No, but it comes to the same thing." For he never lost his union with God, and he used to say that in this life we must pray by our work and action. His own life was certainly an uninterrupted prayer.*

---

* Letter to Dom Jean de Saint-François (December 1623), translated by Elisabeth Stopp in *St. Francis de Sales: A Testimony by St. Chantal* (Hyattsville, MD: Institute of Salesian Studies, 1967), p. 167.

By culling some holy flowers, particularly a word or thought or image taken from a prior meditation, we are able to recall, and thus reactivate, the affections by which we commune with God. (In keeping with the example given above, we could recall the words of the voice from the sky identifying Jesus as the beloved Son, to whom we should listen.) This we can readily do in our minds and hearts even while busy with the other activities of the day.

The second means of praying that St. Francis de Sales recommends is the making of aspirations. As explained in the introduction to part 2 above, these are simple thoughts or brief sayings that we can meditatively call to mind in association with our daily experiences. (So, to continue our example, seeing a mountain or walking up an incline could evoke an aspiration associated with the Transfiguration.) Through these aspirations, we pray even when we are doing other things, as the entire *Spiritual Directory* enjoins us. For the saint, the exercise of making aspirations is crucial to leading a good life, whether in the monastery or in the world. In his view, daily recourse to holy thoughts and words creates a sacred moment that

> can supply the lack of all other prayers, but its loss can hardly be repaired by other means. Without this exercise we cannot properly lead the contemplative life, and we can but poorly lead the active life. Without it rest is mere idleness, and labor is drudgery. (*Introduction*, part 3, chap. 13, p. 92)

By habituating ourselves prayerfully to God's ongoing presence in our world and in our lives, our communing with God endures and is the foretaste of that union we seek to enjoy eternally. Or, to use the linguistic twist that St. Francis de Sales gives it: "We retire into God before we aspire to him, and we aspire to him so that we may retire into him" (*Introduction*, part 3, chap. 13, p. 88). By praying, the life-breathing cycle of aspiration and respiration enables us to live any day well.

12

LIVING THE
"LITTLE VIRTUES"

While St. Francis de Sales considers prayerful communion with God an essential element of the good life, he realizes that living well entails bringing that spiritual transcendence into everyday reality. In his view, the good life is one that is lived, one that is actualized each day in the situations in which we find ourselves, one that seeks to live as best we can and in keeping with the duties of our vocation, or state in life. While we grow affectively through mental prayer, we show it effectively through a life of virtue.

Throughout his writings, St. Francis de Sales, like other spiritual guides, speaks often of the great theological virtues (faith, hope, and love). But, in keeping with his focus on the practicality of the good life, he also emphasizes the practice of those virtues that align with our daily routines and tasks and situations.

Although talk of the virtues is missing from the *Spiritual Directory*, the vast majority of St. Francis de Sales's letters deal with the practice of the good life. And in the third, and lengthiest, part of his *Introduction to the Devout Life*, he treats the practice of virtue explicitly. There he provides instructions on the little virtues, the evangelical counsels, and various social situations in which one can and should lead a virtuous life. To begin, he offers a consideration of which virtues would be best for anyone to put into practice.

For many people, the choice of which virtue to practice often favors the well-known and even heroic ones. Who does not wish to be more courageous? Who would not prefer to be more magnanimous? Who would not like to be in a position to be generous to everyone in need? But the truth of the matter is that most of us will never have the occasion to do tremendous deeds. We may dream of being the one who saves someone's life or changes the world, but our ordinary lives rarely give us the opportunity to do so in such dramatic fashion. Reality is never so ideal.

But reality can always be good. That is why St. Francis de Sales counsels the practice of those virtues we have the opportunity to practice daily and frequently. He shows a preference for those virtues that are better suited to our everyday lives, the ones more "conformable to our duties rather than ... agreeable to our tastes" (*Introduction*, part 3, chap. 1, p. 111).

Among the less-celebrated virtues, he recommends three in particular: humility, gentleness, and simplicity. These "little" virtues may be lowly in terms of not garnering great public esteem; practicing them is not something for which people are widely known. But they are not at all little in terms of being easy to do. Nor are they small in the value they hold for those who practice them. In fact, these are the sort of good deeds that, from the inside out, change lives forever—not only our own but also those with whom we interact each day.

These little virtues make the good life possible and profitable. Each is predicated on the truthfulness of being human. Each has both an exterior and an interior dimension. Each one, properly understood and lived, can counteract a natural proclivity that impedes us from being truly happy. And each of them is eminently doable—though it will take a lifetime of practice!

HUMILITY

The first of the little virtues often gets a bad rap. But unlike in common parlance, humility in the Salesian sense does not refer to humiliation. Rather, humility for St. Francis de Sales means simply an honest estimation of who we are—in both the positive and negative realities of our personal identity. Humility helps us to be sincere and candid when it comes to examining both the good and the bad in our lives.

As the saint explains, humility recognizes, on the one hand, "that none of the good in us comes from ourselves" alone. It sees that the good things about us—our talents, abilities, gifts, et cetera—are all things that we have first received, things that we may have developed but that did not begin by our doing. On the other hand, humility also acknowledges that the bad in us is really there, that our foibles and faults and failings are things for which we are responsible and for which we need to take ownership. Put simply, humility embraces the truth that life is what it is, and we are what we are, although we always try to improve. Humility means seeing ourselves as we stand in relation to God, who created us, for "nothing can so effectively humble us before God's mercy as the multitude of his benefits, and nothing can so deeply humble us before his justice as our countless offenses against him" (*Introduction*, part 3, chap. 5, p. 124) .

Exteriorly, the cultivation of humility is an effective way to counteract pride, that vice that assigns to us the achievement

THE ROAD TO PERFECTION

Dr. M. Scott Peck begins his monumental bestseller, *The Road Less Traveled*,* with one simple sentence: "Life is difficult." His point, demonstrated throughout the book, is that we tend to assume that life should be easier than it is, and we naturally prefer to avoid hardships. To take the "less traveled" road is to learn, through discipline, to confront and solve everyday problems, a way that Peck argues is the only path to happiness

St. Francis de Sales sees it differently. For him, traveling a spiritual road to the good life is difficult not because of avoidance mechanisms but precisely because we wish to be perfect. In the letter cited at the outset of this book, he recognizes how often we desire Christian perfection and even imagine ourselves in this light. But actually putting it into practice remains elusive.

"The desire for a certain kind of Christian perfection ... can be imagined but not carried out, one that many people can talk about but that no one puts into practice" (*Letters of Spiritual Direction*, p. 96). Put in words reminiscent of Peck's introduction, the saint would say that "life needs patience."

Looking at the big picture of our lives, St. Francis de Sales teaches that "patience is the one virtue which gives greatest

---

* M. Scott Peck, *The Road Less Traveled: A New Psychology of Love, Traditional Values, and Spiritual Growth* (New York: Simon and Schuster, 1978). See also his *Further Along the Road Less Traveled* (New York: Simon and Schuster, 1993) and *The Road Less Traveled and Beyond: Spiritual Growth in an Age of Anxiety* (New York: Simon and Schuster, 1997).

assurance of our reaching perfection," and he notes that "while we must have patience with others, we must also have it with ourselves" (*Letters of Spiritual Direction*, p. 96). The reason for this counsel is simple: no one is, or will be, perfect, no matter how much we may want to be or how hard we try to be. In fact, St. Francis says the very desire for perfection often impedes our progress because it leads to flights of spiritual fancy that take us beyond everyday reality, where "we are sometimes so busy being good angels that we neglect to be good men and women" (*Letters of Spiritual Direction*, pp. 97-98).

Thus, while we endeavor to lead more virtuous lives, the saint reminds us that "our imperfections are going to accompany us to the grave. We can't go anywhere without having our feet on the ground" (*Letters of Spiritual Direction*, p. 98). For this reason, he recommends cultivating the little virtues by which we can grow into the good life one step at a time. And that growth begins with each small act of virtue rather than with the desire to make our entire life virtuous.

of what is not, ultimately, our own doing. For example, we may be proud of things we own, especially if we have worked hard to acquire them. But, no matter how fine or fancy or fashionable, these things are not in us; to glory in them is to misplace our honor. St. Francis de Sales explains:

> Some men become proud and overbearing because they ride a fine horse, wear a feather

in their hat, or are dressed in a splendid suit of clothes. Is anyone blind to the folly of all this? If there is any glory in such things it belongs to the horse, the bird, and the tailor. (*Introduction* part 3, chap. 4, p. 121)

So, too, things we can do well are not simply the result of our skills; we may have certain abilities within us, but these are gifts given to us at birth that, with the help of others, we learn to develop. Even if people heap praise or bestow honors on us, humility precludes us from reveling in such esteem. The sort of pride that lurks in classes of rank or places of precedence or titles of honor ends up diminishing the real beauty of who we are, as St. Francis demonstrates with an image from the animal kingdom: "A peacock spreads his tail in self-admiration and by the very act of raising up his beautiful feathers he ruffles all the others and displays [underneath] his own ugliness" (*Introduction*, part 3, chap. 4, p. 122).

Interiorly, the practice of humility focuses on being honest with ourselves and about ourselves. It reveals itself in the ability to laugh at ourselves! "We often say that we are nothing," St. Francis de Sales points out, "but we would be very sorry if anyone took us at our word or told others that we are really such as we say" (*Introduction*, part 3, chap. 4, p. 124). Moreover, we often feel sorry when things do not go the way we want or expect. How many times do we fail despite trying intently to succeed? How often do we say or do something utterly foolish? How frequently do we slip up with no explanation as to why? These are the frailties with which life is fraught. To admit and accept them as our own, despite our desire to be free of them, is to be humble.

Humility grows in us as we increase our thankfulness for all that we have and all that we are. Long before the rise of positive psychology,[55] St. Francis de Sales understood that "a lively consideration of graces received makes us humble because knowledge of them begets gratitude for them" (*Introduction*, part 3, chap. 4, p. 124). Growth in humility also leads to a more courageous bearing with all that happens to us, and even gives us a more daring approach to daily living. As the saint reasons:

> The proud man who trusts in himself has good reason not to attempt anything [that might jeopardize his self-trust]. The humble man is all the more courageous because he recognizes his own impotence. The more wretched he esteems himself the more daring he becomes, because he places his whole trust in God, who rejoices to display his power in our weakness and raise up his mercy in our misery. (*Introduction*, part 3, chap. 4, p. 126)

GENTLENESS

The second of the little virtues that St. Francis de Sales recommends follows from humility as its social counterpart. As the saint puts it, "Humility perfects us with respect to God and meekness with respect to our neighbor" (*Introduction*, part 3, chap. 8, p. 134). Put in other terms, if humility entails being honest

---

[55] See Alexander Pocetto, "Positive Psychology, Francis de Sales, and Character Formation: An Introduction," *Studies in Religion/Sciences Religieuses* 43/4 (2014): 575-591.

about ourselves, gentleness invites us to be honest about, and accepting of, others.[56]

Gentleness follows from humility as a logical consequence. After all, the more we learn to embrace the truth that we are not perfect, the less we will expect or demand that others be perfect toward us. Yet how often do we expect things in life to be different? We expect our technology to function perfectly and speedily. We expect our work to produce positive results in proportion to the effort we put into it. We expect other people to act as we would in the same situation. All too often, and all too easily, we dwell in a world of "should." And when things do not measure up to the image we have in mind, when life does not go as we think it should, or people do not act as we want them to, we often get angry. This powerful emotion, the saint says, "is nourished by a thousand false pretexts," for "there never was an angry man who thought his anger unjust" (*Introduction*, part 3, chap. 8, p. 136).

Exteriorly, we combat the natural, emotional response to life's inevitable downfalls by displaying the twin Salesian virtues: "When humility and meekness are good and true they preserve us from the inflammation and swelling that injuries usually cause in our hearts" (*Introduction*, part 3, chap. 8, p. 135). When we

[56] As Wendy Wright and Joseph Power note in their introduction to the *Letters of Spiritual Direction* (pp. 63-64): "A difficult term to translate, *douceur* has been rendered in English as 'sweetness,' 'gentleness,' 'graciousness,' 'meekness,' and 'suavity.' None of these translations do it full justice.... It connotes an almost maternal quality of serving that is swathed in tender concern. Salesian *douceur* also suggests a sense of being grace-filled, graceful in the broadest use of the term. This gracefulness extends from external demeanor—polite manners and convivial disposition—to the very quality of a person's heart—the way in which a person is interiorly ordered and disposed."

teach ourselves to react with gentleness and to show docility toward those with whom we find fault, our natural passion gives way to a more reasonable response. If, through humility, we are not surprised at our own failings, by gentleness we will not be caught off guard by those we experience in others.

Interiorly, this virtue enables us to be gentle also toward ourselves. In speaking of gentleness in our own regard, St. Francis de Sales identifies an all-too-common experience:

> Although reason requires that we must be displeased and sorry whenever we commit a fault, we must refrain from bitter, gloomy, spiteful, and emotional displeasure. Many people are greatly at fault in this way. When overcome by anger they become angry at being angry, disturbed at being disturbed, and vexed at being vexed. (*Introduction*, part 3, chap. 9, p. 138)

This personal dissatisfaction, as the saint rightly observes, comes from self-love, from a failure to acknowledge our imperfection. All the more reason, then, to cultivate the practice of this second little virtue, of calmly yet firmly, gently yet courageously picking ourselves up and starting anew. As the saint reminds us, "when we have committed some fault, if we rebuke our heart by a calm, mild remonstrance, with more compassion for it than passion against it, and encourage it to make amendment, then repentance conceived in this way will sink far deeper and penetrate more effectually than fretful, angry, stormy repentance" (*Introduction*, part 3, chap. 9, p. 139).

In sum, the Salesian good life entails being nice, toward oneself and toward others. But gentleness is no wishy-washy virtue;

instead, it involves an intentional approach to act not out of emotion (especially anger) but from the realization that others are like we are—imperfect yet worthy, having personal flaws yet also possessing inherent dignity. In this Salesian sense, the practice of docility is demanding, for "nothing is so strong as gentleness—nothing so gentle and loving as real strength." And practically speaking, being nice usually accomplishes more good in the end. To borrow the saint's quaint image, "It takes more oil than vinegar and salt to make a good salad."[57]

SIMPLICITY

The third of the little virtues combines the previous two. When listing the virtues that the good life comprises, St. Francis de Sales most often mentions simplicity. But here again his notion of the term differs from common usage. For this saint, simplicity is not the opposite of complexity. Rather, he intends by this an approach to ourselves, to others, and to life in general that is forthright, plain dealing, and otherwise free from pretense. As Wendy Wright explains:

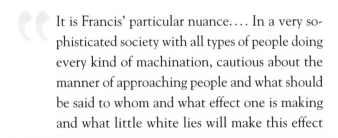

> It is Francis' particular nuance.... In a very so-phisticated society with all types of people doing every kind of machination, cautious about the manner of approaching people and what should be said to whom and what effect one is making and what little white lies will make this effect

---

[57] Both sayings are attributed to St. Francis de Sales by Camus in *The Spirit of St. Francis de Sales* (pp. 11, 185).

and that effect, he says: "No! We must be free
of duplicity, free of guile, free of deceitfulness."[58]

This little virtue runs counter to making things up, to pre-
senting something as other than what it really is. Naturally, we
wish to put our best foot forward in life. Admittedly, we want
others to see only what is good in us. But the desire to "spin"
things that predominates in the world of public relations does not
necessarily correspond to the way things really are. In humility
we embrace what is true about ourselves. In gentleness, we accept
what is true about others. In simplicity, we present ourselves and
see others in an honest light, without feigning anything, without
deceiving, without conspiring, without manipulating the truth
of who we and others are.

Exteriorly, simplicity should govern all our actions, but St.
Francis de Sales often speaks of two particular ways in which
this virtue can characterize our daily comportment. One shows
itself in fashion and the propriety with which we should choose
our attire. Beyond both decency and cleanliness at all times,
how we dress should reflect who we are (e.g., single or married) and should respect the public situation in which we find
ourselves (e.g., a professional setting or a leisurely gathering).
Adding wit to his wisdom, the saint quips: "Old people are
always ridiculous when they try to make themselves pretty.
Such folly can be put up with only in youth" (*Introduction*, part
3, chap. 25, p. 180).

More frequently, the saint speaks of simplicity in terms of
our speech. In his view, our language should always be frank and

---

[58] Wendy Wright, "Simplicity in the Salesian Sources," *Salesian
Living Heritage* (Spring/Fall 1989): 8.

honest, all the while also being charitable. Simplicity also leads us to be reticent when talking about ourselves, as he explains to St. Jane de Chantal:

> Without doubt, whoever speaks little of himself does so extremely well; for, whether it be that we speak in accusing ourselves or in excusing ourselves, in praising ourselves or in despising ourselves, it will always happen that our speech serves to entice us to vanity. If, therefore, some great charity draws us to speak of ourselves and our relatives, we must hold our tongue about it. (*Oeuvres*, vol. 26, pp. 283-294)

Interiorly, simplicity challenges us to render a forthright image of ourselves, one that avoids any prosaic illusions of grandeur that in reality are nothing more than mental temptations. For instance:

> There are souls who make great projects to do excellent services for Our Saviour, by eminent actions and extraordinary sufferings, but actions and sufferings of which there is no opportunity, and perhaps never will be, and who upon this apprehend they have done a great matter in love, in which they are very often deceived — as appears in this, that by embracing in desire, as seems to them, great future crosses, they anxiously avoid the burden of such as are present, which are less. Is it not an extreme temptation to be so valiant in imagination, and so cowardly

in execution? (*Treatise*, book 12, chap. 6, pp. 540-541)

To be simple, instead, is to be cognizant of the opportunities afforded for good that take place in the ordinary responsibilities of our vocation. These everyday tasks are tough enough to handle, without concocting schemes of greater glory! And focusing our attention on our vocational duties will serve to steady us in the struggle to lead a good life. St. Francis de Sales disarms our tendency to self-delusion with this advice: "Take care to manage those little encounters that God presents to you, put in them your virtue, and do not desire great works; for often one lets himself be knocked down by a gnat when he combats monsters by imagination" (*Oeuvres*, vol. 26, p. 36).

The cultivation of simplicity enables us to live the good life, even if, at times, we do not experience the contentment that comes with doing so. By practicing this little virtue, we counteract the deception that our lives should be more meritorious. It also frees us from the false imaginings of a better life elsewhere than in the state in life that is ours, as in the popular proverb that mistakenly suggests that the grass is greener on the other side. The saint says, instead, that "there is no vocation that does not have its trouble, its bitterness, and its distaste." Nevertheless, "[a] person who no longer has the restlessness of his own will is content with everything: provided that God be served, it does not matter in what manner God employs him; provided that he does his divine will, it is all the same to him" (*Oeuvres*, vol. 12, p. 348).

Humility, gentleness, simplicity—with these "little virtues" St. Francis de Sales suggests an ordinary way to live extraordinarily well. Each flows from his everyday sense of spirituality.

LIVE TODAY WELL

Each enables us to be real: by accepting the facts of our human condition, by embracing the truth of our personal character, and by managing the vicissitudes of daily life. By cultivating these virtues, we come to learn that who and what and where we are in God's eyes are really all that matters.

13

CONFESSION AND THE GRACE OF RECONCILIATION

The daily practice of Salesian spirituality—through reintending duties, pausing for prayer, and exercising the little virtues—makes for a good life. But beyond what we can do each day, other sacred moments bring into focus what God does for us. These are the sacraments, two of which St. Francis de Sales highlights in the *Spiritual Directory* and in his other writings.

For St. Francis the sacrament of Reconciliation (aka Confession) affords us the opportunity to experience divine compassion directly. In a "memo" in which he provides pastoral advice about Confession to the priests in his diocese, the saint emphasizes the sacrament's salutary power. He reckons that "confession and penance render a man infinitely more honorable than sin renders him blamable" and that "the greater our misery, the more is the mercy of God glorified."[59] With this attitude in mind, we might approach the sacrament more frequently and more profitably.

---

[59] St. Francis de Sales, "Advice to Confessors," *Oeuvres*, vol. 23, pp. 279-298. English translation by Joseph M. Baraniewicz published

In the lifelong fight against our faults, the aid of divine grace is indispensable. To avail ourselves of this heavenly help through sacramental means, St. Francis de Sales recommends first that we prepare thoroughly to receive it. In the *Spiritual Directory*, he suggests several ways by which to ready ourselves for Confession. First:

> In the spirit of deep humility at the feet of our crucified Lord, we will ask for the grace and light of the Holy Spirit to discern our faults well.

Here the image evokes the intention. Coming to grips with the theology of atonement — in which Christ's death on the Cross responds to the deadly nature of sin for all humanity — we first humble ourselves with the consideration that our own sins contribute to what Christ suffered. This little virtue grows larger through spiritual imagination: were we to stand "at the feet of our crucified Lord," how could we not be moved to repentance?

Coupled with this excitement of our affections, a cognitional preparation is also needed. To this end we acknowledge that, given our natural aversion to self-recrimination, we need help to know ourselves well and thereby discern what is really going on in the faults we commit. We call on the aid of a spiritual light, to shine on our deeds in such a way that we can see them not simply from our own perspective but from God's. In this way we will see more clearly that we stand always in need of divine grace.

Then, with hearts and minds opened to reconciliation:

---

by the Institute of Salesian Studies and made available online by the Salesian Center for Faith and Culture at DeSales University.

We should recall everything we have found in our daily examinations since our previous confession and consider for a moment if there is anything else.

This act of personal recall presumes the daily practice of the Examen (explained in chapter 9). It also supposes a much more frequent practice of sacramental Confession than is common today. Otherwise, such total recall of *everything* we have done would be virtually impossible! Even then, the saint recognizes that we must think about this twice — in case there is anything else we might have missed, given the fickleness of our memories.

Still, recalling actual faults is necessary, no matter the length of time since our previous confession. For St. Francis de Sales, this realistic appraisal arises not simply as supplying the traditional "matter" of the sacrament, but as coming from the everyday focus of our spiritual quest. Just as our devotion is to be enacted in concrete deeds, so our failings take shape in actual times and places and affect real people. Even if we are unable to recall everything, the examination of conscience the saint calls for here is not a generalized view or broad perspective. Rather, he invites us to give humble consideration to the actual what and when and where of how we live, particularly when we do not live as well as we ought or as we would like.

After this, let us humbly ask Our Lord for pardon and for the grace to correct ourselves. For this purpose we will make a firm resolution, especially concerning the more important things we have noticed.

PROFITING FROM OUR FAULTS*

Leading a good life can be a struggle. Failures happen. Faults persist. As a result, futility frustrates our never-ending quest to become better people. For St. Francis de Sales, however, even when we fail, we can find an opportunity for growth. To profit from our faults, he proposes a three-step process.

It begins with the recognition of the uphill struggle we face in life. In truth, he says, "we must never be astonished at finding ourselves imperfect ... because there is no cure for it" (pp. 101-102). Human finitude limits the personal resolve even of saints, as he writes to St. Jane de Chantal: "I don't know how I am made. I feel miserable, but I don't trouble myself about it; and sometimes I am even happy in thinking that I am a really good object for the mercy of God" (pp. 92-93).

Admitting our inability to keep our resolutions is good; despairing about this is not. No one likes failure, but our typical responses to it—either giving up or trying harder—do not change the fact that earthly perfection eludes us. This is why the saint repeatedly counsels calmness amid the calamities of life. "When we discover that the lute is out of tune, it isn't necessary to break its strings and throw it out! What we have to do is to lend an attentive ear to discover which is the discordant string, and then tighten or loosen it as required" (p. 38). When we show "more compassion for [our heart] than passion against it," the potential

---

* Joseph Tissot, *How to Profit from Your Faults: Based on the Writings of St. Francis de Sales* (New York: Scepter, 2004).

for change "will sink far deeper and penetrate more effectively than fretful, angry, stormy repentance" (p. 29).

Step two is to shift the balance of power by focusing not on our own ineptitude but on the eternal power of God. After all, no matter the prevalence of our misdeeds, nothing that we do or fail to do can change who God is or what God does for us. "The foundation of [our] trust," he writes, "should be in him, not in us. All the more so because we change, and he never does; he always remains good and merciful, whether we are weak and imperfect or whether we are strong and perfect" (pp. 87-88).

Having handed our efforts over to this saving God, all that remains, as the final step, is to begin again … and again and again! In Salesian spirituality, renewing our resolutions is not a sign of desperation but of persistence. Starting over despite never seeming to arrive at our goal comes not from being thickheaded but from being faithful and hopeful. To this end, the saintly Doctor encourages us: "Rest is reserved for heaven … [while] on earth we should always fight as though we are between fear and hope. But we must do so, knowing that hope will always be the stronger, bearing in mind the power of the One who comes to our aid" (p. 98).

Acknowledging wrong is hard. But humility is good, and so is God's mercy. To ask God for pardon and grace is to redirect our intention to our Lord rather than to wallow in our imperfection. This prayerful request turns us away from ourselves and toward God, who alone leads us along the way of the good life.

To advance on that never-ending path:

> We will renounce our faults and attempt to stir up true sorrow for them, however slight they may be, because it is always too great an evil to have been displeasing to the sovereign goodness of our Savior who is so merciful to us each day.

This dual response—an effective renunciation and an affective sorrow—results from the foregoing considerations. An honest consideration of our thoughts and words and deeds in light of God's love for us can yield only a displeasing recognition: we fail in our relationship to God and others. But, as St. Francis de Sales learned at a young age, this admission need not beget depression. Instead, the merciful goodness of God remains sovereign—and is magnanimously offered to us each day.

With this salvation in mind, one preparatory step remains:

> Having noticed our current faults, we should add something from the past which is clearly sinful and make an act of contrition for all these together.

Why add some past sin to our list? Are our current faults and failings not sufficient to engender humility and sorrow? What St. Francis de Sales recommends here does not deny the efficacy of sacramental confession to absolve all sins in our life, even those we cannot recall. Rather, it serves simply as a powerful reminder that imperfection accompanies us throughout this life. Still, the saint acknowledges this human reality positively: "Dear imperfections, they force us to acknowledge our misery, give us practice in humility, selflessness, patience, and watchfulness; yet, notwithstanding, God looks at the preparation of our heart and sees that it is perfect" (*Letters of Spiritual Direction*, p. 98).

The time of preparation is now complete. While it appears long and detailed, it need not be so in practice. This preparation can take place in a short period spent in quiet prayer, particularly if we have accustomed ourselves to this self-examination on a regular basis. With this humble recognition, sorrowful affection, and renewed resolution in mind:

> Then we will go humbly to our confessor honoring God and the sacred priesthood in the person of the priest. We ought to look upon him in confession as an angel whom God sends to reconcile us to his divine goodness.

Here, it seems, is where the celebration of this sacrament has run into difficulty. A common objection today asks why we should confess our sins to a priest instead of entreating God's forgiveness directly from the Almighty. Particularly if one has had a bad experience in the confessional, this element of the divine-human interaction becomes an obstacle to the reconciliation we seek.

Sadly, that experience is all too real. Logically, the objection appears legitimate. But if we were to consider the process on a purely human level, we can come to understand why this sacramental process works in parallel fashion. When we wrong someone we love, our own recognition of what we have done and our own hope that we will be forgiven does not suffice to right the wrong. We must admit to the beloved our own culpability and express our sorrow for having harmed the relationship. And when we hear the one we love express forgiveness, we know for sure that our harmful deed is relegated to the past; then, and only then, does our reconciliation really begin.

So, too, when that reconciliation takes place with God. In St. Francis de Sales's words, we honor this process in the humble recognition that this sacrament is the ordinary means of experiencing divine reconciliation, as established by the Lord himself in his commissioning of the disciples to forgive sins in God's name. We may be able to speak directly to God, and we should; after all, it is to God, not a priest, that we confess our sins and express our sorrow. But in our limited human state, the other side of the conversation remains imperceptible; we cannot hear the divine response directly, as we would in a human relationship. Yet the concrete experience of forgiveness requires that we "sense" it, that we hear the words, that we know it to be so.

This is the role the priest plays. As St. Francis de Sales pictures it, the priest is the "angel whom God sends" to make this forgiveness real and enable divine reconciliation to be experienced. By this, the saint is not describing the priest's personal character! In fact, he advises confessors to assure the one who comes to confession "that you are not an angel, no more than he is" ("Advice to Confessors," p. 3). Instead, what is "angelic" in this image is the need for, and process of, mediation: just as angels serve to communicate a divine message, so the priest conveys divine mercy in human words that we are able to hear and understand. To emphasize this interactive reality, St. Francis de Sales has strong words for the priest in the confessional. In addition to pointing out that "ordinarily it is better to treat the penitent with love and mildness ... than to treat him sharply" ("Advice to Confessors," p. 8), he advises them to

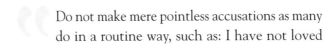

> remember that at the beginning of their confes-
> sions the poor penitents call you Father, and that
> you must indeed have a fatherly heart towards
> them, receiving them with a great charity,
> bearing patiently their uncouthness, ignorance,
> weakness, slowness, and other imperfections.
> Never leave off aiding them and assisting them
> as long as there is hope of their amendment.
> ("Advice to Confessors," p. 3)

In the *Spiritual Directory*, St. Francis de Sales also explains the penitent's side of the conversation:

> Let us be brief and clear in our confession. Let us
> never confess out of routine or scrupulosity, but
> rather out of devotion and attention as in an action
> of great importance and value.

With this counsel, he expresses the nature of and the motivation behind the conversation that takes place in the sacrament. His call for brevity suggests that this dialogue differs from that of a coun-seling session; after all, God already knows what we have done or failed to do. St. Francis's call for clarity is simply practical; the reconciliation process, as in any earthly encounter, requires knowl-edge of what is really going on in the divine-human relationship.

In his *Introduction*, St. Francis provides further insight. To assist us with being clear in our confession, he says:

> Do not make mere pointless accusations as many
> do in a routine way, such as: I have not loved

God as much as I should; I have not prayed with as much devotion as I should; I have not loved my neighbor as I should; I have not received the sacraments as reverently as I should, and the like. The reason is that when you say such things you say nothing definite to help your confessor know your state of conscience. Every saint in heaven and every man on earth might say the same thing if they went to confession. (*Introduction*, part 2, chap. 19, p. 102)

Instead, he suggests that we not only confess what we have done (or failed to do), but, more importantly, that we acknowledge the reason for it and the motive behind it. These are what allow us to see ourselves as we really are and become the place where we focus renewed energy, with the help of divine grace, in becoming who we are called to be.

This, ultimately, is the point of going to Confession. Engaging in this penitential dialogue can improve our self-understanding through the process of acknowledging where we still need to grow. It also affords us a chance to "practice the virtues of humility, obedience, simplicity, and charity" in a way that surpasses any other act (*Introduction*, part 2, chap. 19, p. 101). But the real benefit to the sacramental celebration comes in the opportunity it gives us to encounter God and experience divine grace. In hearing the words of absolution, we know directly and concretely that our sins have been forgiven, that our faults "are buried before God and the confessor in such a way that they will never be remembered" ("Advice to Confessors," p. 3). And on account of this sacred moment of never-ending mercy, we can "go in peace"—to begin again, one step farther along the path to the good life.

14

MASS AND THE GRACE OF ENCOUNTER

The experience of divine grace that the sacraments confer comes to a high point in the celebration of the Mass, where we encounter Jesus really present to us and for us. For St. Francis de Sales this sacred moment is paramount, and sharing in Holy Communion offers the greatest means of growing in the good life.

Prefiguring, as it were, the Church's view of the Eucharist as the "source and summit of the life and mission of the Church,"[60] St. Francis de Sales's estimation of the liturgical celebration of this sacrament is downright effusive. For him, this sacred moment is

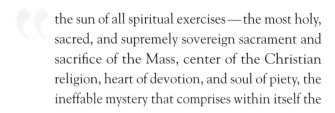

> the sun of all spiritual exercises — the most holy, sacred, and supremely sovereign sacrament and sacrifice of the Mass, center of the Christian religion, heart of devotion, and soul of piety, the ineffable mystery that comprises within itself the

---

[60] This theme was explored in the XI Ordinary General Assembly of the Synod of Bishops in 2004.

> deepest depths of divine charity, the mystery in
> which God really gives himself and gloriously
> communicates his graces and favors to us. (*In-
> troduction*, part 2, chap. 14, p. 92)

As light is necessary for life, so the Mass is the Church's sun. But
unlike anything else in the cosmos, this sacrament celebrates
what is supremely sovereign; as a sacred moment, it is set apart
(the root meaning of *holy*) in both time and place, for it celebrates God's doing, not ours. That divine action is sacrificial,
because the liturgy memorializes Christ's redemptive death on
the Cross on behalf of mankind. The Mass thus becomes the
center of the Christian religion, for by this work the Church
enacts God's salvific presence in the world's midst. As the heart
of devotion, this presence enlivens us from within; as the soul
of piety, it touches on and transforms that which is profoundly
spiritual about being human. Being fundamentally spiritual, not
social, the liturgy is mysterious; it "works" through the ineffable
power of divine grace. It discloses the deepest depths of charity inasmuch as it re-presents the divine condescension on our
behalf. In this we see and hear and experience again the gift of
God's sharing the grace and favor of his eternal love with us.

In the *Spiritual Directory*, St. Francis de Sales dedicates two
articles to this topic: one on the Mass and one on Holy Communion. In them we find the distinctive Salesian emphasis on
interiority as the foundation of spiritual experience and the
eminently practical approach to living the devout life by way of
considerations, affections, and resolutions. In these articles, the
saint anticipates the Church's concern for the fully conscious
and active participation of all in the liturgical assembly, and
he correctly explains how this participation is to be actualized.

Given the risk, then as now, of seeing the Mass as a passive exercise on the part of worshippers,[61] St. Francis de Sales urges all who participate in the liturgy actually to be engaged through the very faculties that make us who we are — namely, our minds and our hearts. He begins with the same admonition that he counsels whenever we begin to pray or seek to commune with the divine:

> First of all we should place ourselves in the presence of God.

Recalling that the Mass is primarily about God's action, and not merely a human interaction, the saint then suggests concrete ways to be attuned to this divine presence throughout the liturgy.

> When the celebrant invites the faithful to repentance we should acknowledge our sins, be truly sorry for them, and ask God's pardon.

Following the liturgical greeting, the first element in the Introductory Rites is the expression of repentance in light of our fundamental unworthiness to participate in this divine act and of the magnanimous gift of God's mercy. The formulary words of the assembly — "I confess . . ." and "Lord, have mercy" — express this

---

[61] In Francis's time, Mass would have been celebrated through words spoken and actions done entirely by the priest-celebrant and the ministers at the altar. In fact, his counsels in the *Spiritual Directory* and in the *Introduction to the Devout Life* fall under the heading of "how to *hear* Mass." Nevertheless, his advice expounds on an "active" sense of worship even then.

sorrow and request for God's pardon. Thus, in Salesian spirituality, our participation in the Mass comes about first by intending the words we say rightly and fully.

This intentional speech turns to attentive listening in the Liturgy of the Word. St. Francis de Sales also advises that we participate with the celebrant in prayerfully appropriating the Good News that is proclaimed at this point in the liturgy:

> At the Gospel, we will rise promptly to give witness to the fact that we are ready to walk in the way of its precepts, saying interiorly:
>
> *Jesus Christ was made obedient to death, even to death on the cross. (Phil 2:8)*
>
> As we make the Sign of the Cross, we will declare:
>
> *May God be in my mind, on my lips, and in my heart, that I may accept his holy Gospel.*

The singing of the Gospel acclamation ("alleluia") signals not only a change in posture but a call to arise in the sense of discipleship. Here lies the Salesian genius — the simple act of standing can itself be an act of worship, if we intend it so as a witness to our personal desire to follow Christ and walk in his ways. This biblical aspiration, or others we may say, is something easy to recall and consider as we get up from our seats. Similarly, in the act of making the Sign of the Cross on our forehead, mouth, and breast, we can speak interiorly the words that correspond to our baptismal choice to follow the Lord.

This emphasis on discipleship expressed interiorly continues with our recitation of the Creed.

> If the Profession of Faith is to be said, we should
> recite it affirming interiorly our willingness to live
> and die in the belief of the Church.

Again, St. Francis de Sales seeks to unite the spiritual (willingness) with the material (words), the interior and the exterior. The words carry great meaning, however rote they may have become. The Profession of Faith is the verbal standard by which we bear witness before others to the substantive content of what we believe. To be willing "to live and die" for what those words mean constitutes a real profession of who we are; considering the theological speech-act in this way lends significance to what otherwise could simply be an exercise in memorization.

The saint then considers the Liturgy of the Eucharist and, first, the great prayer that tells the story of our salvation.

> After the Sanctus [Holy, Holy, Holy] we should
> very humbly and reverently reflect on the blessings
> conferred by the passion and death of our Savior. We
> ought to implore him to will their application to the
> salvation of the whole world, especially to our own
> and that of all the members of the Church, for the
> glory and happiness of all the saints and for the relief
> of the souls in purgatory.

Here again, Salesian spirituality seeks to unite bodily movement and spiritual intention. After the Sanctus, the assembly kneels—a gesture of humility and reverence. Depending on the quality of the architecture, it might even be uncomfortable! But even that can aid in reflecting on the blessing we have received through the Passion and death of our Savior, narratively referred to at this point in the liturgy. In this prayer position, while attuned to the words being said and the story being told, we pray with the celebrant. Each version of the Eucharistic Prayer includes petitions for our salvation and that of the Church and the world. We honor the saints and seek spiritual aid for the deceased souls. In all this we actively participate by attentively listening to and intentionally focusing on the actions being spoken about in the Eucharistic Prayer.

At the elevation of the Blessed Sacrament, we are to adore it with deep contrition of heart. Then we will offer it with the celebrant to God the Father for the remission of our own sins and those of the whole world, and offer ourselves with the priest and the entire Church. After the elevation we will thank Jesus Christ for his passion and for the institution of this Holy Sacrifice of the Altar.

In this midst of the Eucharistic Prayer, following the Consecration, the elevation of the Blessed Sacrament takes place. This pause in the narration calls for everyone to look up, literally and figuratively. That gaze enacts our adoration of the Lord and Savior eternally above us yet now really present before us. Our response, quite naturally, is one of deep contrition, for no one is worthy to be in such close proximity to the divine presence. We acknowledge, usually with a sung acclamation, that in this mystery of faith is found humanity's salvation, in the remission of sins that has been memorialized in the liturgy. We offer ourselves to

God in this moment by making that acclamation self-referential: we are truly the ones who proclaim the Lord's death, profess the Resurrection, await his coming again, and receive the gift of salvation that sets us free. The remainder of the Eucharistic Prayer expresses thanks for what is offered here — namely, the Passion of Jesus Christ — and makes prayerful petition for those in the Mystical Body of the entire Church: those here below (the clergy and the laity) and all those who have gone before us in death.

The Communion Rite then begins with the recitation of the Lord's Prayer, which provides another opportunity for our active participation in the liturgical action.

> When the celebrant says the "Our Father," we will say it with him with great humility and devotion just as if we were hearing him saying it to the Father and we were repeating it word for word with him.

The image St. Francis de Sales proposes here helps to recall, and in a sense reenact, the origins of this prayer, in which the disciples asked Jesus to teach them how to pray.

Following the sign of peace and the Lamb of God, we then come to the time of actual communion with God. To make our participation in this act fully conscious, St. Francis de Sales proposes the same dynamic of considerations, affections, and resolutions that elsewhere he counsels as the method for mental prayer. These elements correspond to what we do before receiving, at the moment of receiving, and after receiving Holy Communion.

The actual reception of this sacrament is not something difficult. In fact, it can be quite routine: we extend our hand or tongue, and we receive it, in the material sense. But to "get it" in the spiritual sense does require preparation on our part.[62] To combat the tendency simply to go through the liturgical motions, St. Francis de Sales counsels us, first, to give consideration to what is really taking place.

> The principal intention which we should have at Holy Communion is union with Our Lord.

Prior to receiving the sacrament, in the time before we even leave our seats, we can raise our consciousness to the realization that this is, indeed, the Body of Christ. By directing our intention toward being united with our Lord, we rightly recognize this sacrament for the divine-human encounter that it is.

> To prepare ourselves better for this union, it would be good in our prayer and recollection to raise our thoughts somewhat to Our Lord in this sacrament. We should stir up in our soul a holy reverence and spiritual joy that we should be so blessed as to receive our gentle Savior. Then we ought to renew our decision to serve him fervently. When we have received him, we can reaffirm this decision by a good and holy resolution.

[62] In "A Little Treatise on Holy Communion," which St. Francis de Sales wrote for the abbess of a Benedictine convent (*Oeuvres*, vol. 26, pp. 211-223), he suggests a more detailed process of preparation in terms of cleansing our understanding (of curiosities), our memory (of worldly goods), and our will (of disordered affections) and adorning the same three faculties with a desire for the blessing of real communion with God.

While, again, the saint's advice here sounds painstaking, it need not be. In the simple act of walking forward to receive Communion, we can direct our thoughts to what awaits us. When we consider what is really happening — that our God is about to come to us in this sacrament — we cannot help but experience reverence and joy within. In response to this blessing we are about to receive, we can intentionally renew the decision to be his disciples and serve him fervently in our lives.

Then the sacred moment arrives when we receive our Lord and are united with Him. The moment itself is fleeting; it takes just a quick swallow, a short turn, and we walk back to our seats. To transform this ordinary routine into a sacred experience, St. Francis de Sales again counsels the use of prayerful aspirations:

At the moment of communion, we could use some mental or vocal aspiration, such as that of St. Francis:

Who am I, Lord, and who are you?

or perhaps that of St. Elizabeth:

Where does this blessing come from — that my Lord should come to me? (Luke 1:43)

or that of St. John the Evangelist:

Yes, come, Lord Jesus. (Rev. 22:20)

As always, the actual thought or saying can be anything that helps us to focus on the moment immediately before us. The scriptural aspirations proposed by the saint are typical responses to the recognition that what appears to be bread and wine actually is the presence of our Lord.

Then, in the time that follows our reception of the sacrament, we can really commune with God. Here again, the sensible moment (i.e., the taste or act of digestion) can pass quickly. For this reason, it takes an intentional act on our part to appreciate the real presence of God now within us:

> After Holy Communion, we should consider Our Lord seated in our heart as on his throne and bring before him, one after the other, our faculties and senses to hear his commands and promise him fidelity.

In the silence of our souls (which requires also a time of silence during this part of the liturgy), we use our interior "faculties and senses" to give greater attention to what has just transpired. In this sacrament, God really is present, and in our reception of the sacrament, God really has come into us. In pondering the full reality of that supernatural presence, we can stir our hearts to a variety of holy affections. Some that the saint suggests are:

> Fear of displeasing and losing the Lord:
> *My Lord, be not far from me. (Ps. 38:22)*
>
> or, as the travelers on the road to Emmaus:
> *Stay with us, for it is nearly evening. (Luke 24:29)*

Confidence and courage:
I will fear no evil because you are at my side, Lord. (Ps. 23:4)

Love:
My lover belongs to me and I to him; he will rest in my heart; I have found him whom my heart loves. I will not let him go. (Song of Songs 2:16; 1:13; 3:4)

Thanksgiving:
O Lord, because you have given me this great grace, I will bless you eternally and forever, and I will make your praises as countless as the stars of the sky. (Gen. 22:16-19)

Determination to serve the Lord (the words of Jacob):
The Lord shall be my God, and the stone of my heart, heretofore hardened, will be his abode. (Gen. 28:21-22)

Or, as the saint also suggests, we can think of ourselves as being in this moment in the same state as that of Mary, who literally carried the Lord within her, and we can respond accordingly:

We can also think of the interior fervor of our Lady, her devotion, her humility, her confidence and her courage when the angel told her that the Holy Spirit would come into her. We can recall, too, that at the same time that she understood that God was giving her his heart, namely, his Son, she in turn gave herself to God and her soul was overwhelmed with love. We, too, receive a similar grace in Communion. It is not an angel, but Jesus Christ himself who assures us that in this action the Holy Spirit comes into us and in a way Christ is conceived and born in us. O God, what delight and peace!

Consequently after this consideration the soul can truly say as did this holy Lady:

I am the servant of the Lord. Let it be done to me according to his word which he spoke from his sacred mouth, that whoever feeds on him remains in him and he in them, and that whoever feeds on him will live for him, by him and in him and will live forever. (Luke 1:38; John 6:50, 55-59)

The saint's lengthy explanation of how to prepare for and be attuned to the presence of God in this sacrament leads to the same resolution as Mary's—our own fiat in renewing our commitment in faith to be the Lord's disciples. This, ultimately, is what we mean when we say *amen*. In that single word meaning "so be it," we declare our belief that this truly is the Body of Christ. We affirm that to which we aspire in our communal desire to be the Body of Christ. And we resolve that this sacred moment is the one to which our entire life is drawn, here sacramentally and eternally in heaven—namely, that we be united with our Lord. In this way, the Mass recalls and reenacts the Good News of salvation that is the entire story of the Gospel.

LITURGICAL THEOPOETICS*

As a Counter-Reformation bishop, St. Francis de Sales wrote extensively about the doctrine of the Eucharist. But his pastoral genius is more "theopoetic"—in his focus on the disclosure of the divine in and through the crucial nexus of the sacrament. With his profoundly spiritual imagination, he sees our encounter with God in the Eucharist as mirroring key moments in the Gospel narrative.

On the Annunciation: in both mysteries we find Jesus "who, in order to unite himself to us, abandoned and gently abased himself, even to rendering himself food and nourishment for us who are the nutriment and food of worms" (*Oeuvres* XVIII:400).

On the virginal conception: in imitation of Mary, "contentment may be practiced by imitation, among those who, having communicated, feel by the certainty of faith that which, not flesh and blood, but the Heavenly Father has revealed, that their Saviour is body and soul present, with a most real presence, to their body and to their soul, by this most adorable sacrament" (*Treatise*, book 6, chap. 7, pp. 252-253).

On the Visitation: he says to the Sisters who bear the name of this event, "how you should be overwhelmed with joy when you are visited by this Divine Savior in the Most Blessed Sacrament of the Altar, and by the interior graces which you receive

* Thomas F. Dailey, O.S.F.S., "Eucharist and the Theopoetics of Encounter according to St. Francis de Sales," in J. Chorpenning, O.S.F.S., ed., *Human Encounter in the Salesian Tradition* (Rome: International Commission on Salesian Studies, 2007), pp. 63-76.

daily from His Divine Majesty through the many inspirations and words which He speaks to your hearts."*

On the public ministry: at Cana "in His first miracle [Jesus] changed water into wine; and in the last one which He performed before His death He instituted the Eucharist, the Sacrament of His true presence.... This truth may contradict our senses, which perceive nothing of its reality. Yet we believe it—and even believe it with greater delight the more our senses fail us here."**

On the Passion: "the Eucharist represents it principally on account of the total identity of the one who is offered there and of him who was offered on the cross, who is none other than Jesus Christ" (*Oeuvres* II:216).

On the Resurrection: "he will come out of the sepulchre really but in an invisible manner," and later "you will see Christ the pilgrim making a journey without being recognized. The body of Christ is thus in the Eucharist, and not only his body, but also his blood, his living and vivifying soul and his divinity" (*Sermons for Advent and Christmas*, p. 107).

On the Ascension: "See, in effect, I pray you, this body, no longer carnal, but spiritual, which penetrates the heavens" (*Oeuvres*, vol. 8, p. 24).

* *The Sermons of St. Francis de Sales on Our Lady*, ed. Lewis Fiorelli, trans. Nuns of the Visitation (Rockford, IL: TAN Books, 1985), p. 59.
** *The Sermons of St. Francis de Sales for Advent and Christmas*, ed. Lewis Fiorelli, trans. Nuns of the Visitation (Rockford, IL: TAN Books, 1987), p. 107.

Thus does St. Francis de Sales appreciate the Eucharist through the Gospel, and the Gospel through the sacrament. Here Jesus is truly alive and really present to us, in order that we might be united to him. This divine encounter is what we experience whenever we receive Holy Communion.

Following the reception of the sacrament, the liturgy concludes with a prayerful sending forth of the congregation into the world. To appreciate this Concluding Rite, St. Francis de Sales bids us one last consideration in his *Spiritual Directory*:

> At the blessing we should recall that Jesus Christ is giving us his blessing at the same time.

Divinely blessed in this sacred moment of the liturgical celebration of the Mass and in the reception of Holy Communion, we are empowered anew to live the good life.

THE UNIVERSAL CALL TO HOLINESS

In his *Spiritual Directory*, and throughout his writings, St. Francis de Sales offers a detailed, yet doable way to lead a good life. This present-day guide attempts to capture the saint's genius and introduce his thought to readers who seek to live their faith well in the midst of the world. This faith-filled life embodies the universal call to holiness that rang out at the Second Vatican Council. The council's Dogmatic Constitution on the Church sounds a high note concerning the essential role to be played by the laity in the Church and in the world:

> The laity, by their very vocation, seek the king-dom of God by engaging in temporal affairs and by ordering them according to the plan of God. They live in the world, that is, in each and in all of the secular professions and occupations. They live in the ordinary circumstances of fam-ily and social life, from which the very web of their existence is woven. They are called there by God that by exercising their proper function

and led by the spirit of the Gospel they may work
for the sanctification of the world from within as
a leaven. (*Lumen Gentium*, no. 31)

That sanctification comes about in the world, but not by the power of the world. Instead, as St. Francis de Sales lived and taught, we work toward it by gradually becoming who we are in God's eyes and being that perfectly (the theme of part 1 of this book). The interiority of the divine call precedes the living out of holiness in the human works that we do. To show the Salesian way of responding to that call of grace so as to transform all that we do is the purpose of this guide.

Personal transformation, and through it the sanctification of society, is an ongoing process; living a spiritually good life requires continual effort. Yet it is possible! According to St. Francis de Sales, this can happen by developing two faculties: our attention and our intention. On the one hand, we can learn to be more and more attuned to the presence of God in the activities and events of our everyday lives. On the other hand, we learn to decide and resolve, ever more humbly and gently and firmly, to live each day as well as we can.

Thus, contrary to a contemporary view of religious faith as an escape from reality through delusional flights of fancy, Salesian spirituality helps us to cultivate the mystical and the divine amid what is otherwise mundane and merely human. This we do, as explained earlier, by uniting ourselves to God's will both in the ordinary routines of each day (part 2) and in the sacred moments of our lives (part 3).

As suggested at the outset, this spiritual insight, which owes its origin and development to a saint named Francis, finds its continuation today in a pope named Francis. The Holy Father's continuing worldwide appeal no doubt comes from his ability to touch the hearts of all people, whatever their personal circumstances might be, with a message of mercy and an invitation to live joyfully. We see evidence of this in a recent general audience (on November 14, 2014) in which Pope Francis spoke about the universal call to holiness with his characteristic spontaneity and directness. There, too, we heard an echo of the Salesian spirituality explored in this book.

The fundamental premise of St. Francis de Sales's *Introduction to the Devout Life* is that the good life is not limited to those in ordained ministries or religious orders. So, too, the pope declares that "holiness is not the prerogative of only a few: holiness is a gift that is offered to all, without exception, so that it constitutes the distinctive character of every Christian."

The guiding principle of St. Francis de Sales's *Spiritual Directory* affirms that each day offers us multiple opportunities to embody and enact the Faith we profess. So, too, Pope Francis insists that "indeed, it is by living with love and offering Christian witness in our daily tasks that we are called to become saints."

The constant theme of St. Francis de Sales's pastoral letters centers on the idea that holiness is not something separate from or added to daily responsibilities; rather, it is the good life lived in and through the vocation to which God calls us. So, too, the pope explains that "at home, on the streets, at work, at church, in the moment and with the state of life that you have, a door is opened on the road to sainthood. Do not be discouraged to travel this road. God gives [us] the grace to do so."

And the prevailing sentiment of St. Francis de Sales in all his writings is an optimism that sees human fulfillment not in what we do for ourselves, but as a consequence of the eternal love of God, demonstrated to us in his Son and Holy Spirit, and the corresponding love of God that we show to one another. So, too, the pope concludes his message with this optimistic outlook: "When the Lord calls us to be saints, he does not call us to something hard or sad. Not at all! It is an invitation to share His joy, to live and offer every moment of our lives with joy, at the same time making it a gift of love for the people around us."

The words of Pope Francis continue to invite the world to live with joy, hope, and charity for all. The thoughts of St. Francis de Sales offer people of faith a way to respond to that invitation. May this guide to the good life help us all to *live today well.*

Appendix 1

The Spiritual Directory

Preface

Come, O sons blessed from all eternity, and as was said to Ezekiel and to St. John the Evangelist; Come, take hold of this book and eat it, swallow it, fill your heart and nourish your soul with it. Let its words remain day and night before your eyes that you may meditate on them and in your hands that you may put them into practice, and let your entire being praise God for them. This book will prove bitter to your interior, for it will lead to the perfect mortification of your self-love. It will, on the other hand, be sweeter than honey in your mouth because there is no consolation equal to that of mortifying our self-love in order to let live and reign in us the love of him who died for love of us. In this way your bitterness will be transformed into the sweetness of a perfect peace, and you will be filled with true happiness.

I ask you, my sons, nay rather I beg and exhort you, be strong, firm, persevering, unchanging and so remain in order that nothing may separate you from Jesus Christ who has brought you together, nor from that community which can keep you one with him, so that, all of you having but one heart and one mind, he himself may be your only mind and heart.

Blessed the man who lives this Rule, for it is reliable and true. May the grace, peace and consolation of the Holy Spirit be given abundantly and forever to all who follow it, Amen.

Live Jesus!

Intentions and Wishes of Our Holy Father

The intention of our holy Father was that our whole life and all our works be dedicated to union with God, so that we might assist in the renewal of the Church and the salvation of our neighbor by our prayer, works, and good example, and that we might excel in every kind of virtue — this he desired more than anything else.

This desire drew from his fatherly heart, aflame with the zeal of the Holy Spirit, the following three wishes, which he wrote on the first pages of the Profession Book.

The Humble Glory of the Congregation

We have no bond but the bond of love, which is the bond of perfection. For stern as death is love, relentless as the nether world is devotion. How then could there be any bond stronger than the bond of love, which is the bond of perfection?

The love of Jesus Christ impels us.

Prayer to Jesus Christ Our Lord

O true God, who will grant me so great a favor that the Almighty heed my wish and himself write this book, so that I may wear it over my shoulder like a cloak and place it on my head like a crown, that I may proclaim it at each step and offer it to him as to a king?

Yes, Lord Jesus, listen to the cry my heart makes for those in your service: you, yourself write in this book. Never allow anyone to put his name in it except by your inspiration and invitation, so that it may be a cloak of honor on my shoulders and a crown of glory on my head. Thus in all my prayers to you I will mention the names written therein as a song of joy and praise, and offer the list of them as a fragrant bouquet to your divine providence.

Grant, O Jesus, that the year in which each Oblate writes his offering in this book be for him a year of sanctification; the day, a day of salvation; the hour, an hour of lasting blessing. May the hearts which you have brought together in your name and in that of your dear Mother be not scattered, those you have called together be not dispersed, and those you have joined together be not separated. Grant rather that the names found on these perishable pages be written forever in the *Book of the Living* with the just who reign with you in the life of unceasing happiness. So be it. Amen.

Wish Addressed to the Members of the Congregation

Therefore, my brothers and sons whom I love and long for, you who are my joy and my crown, continue, my dear ones, to stand firm in the Lord. I invite you, I even implore all of you to have one and the same love and to live in common accord about this vocation in Jesus Christ, Our Lord, and in his Mother, our Lady. Amen.

Francis, Bishop of Geneva (Annecy, 1611)

Article 1

Rising

First of all on awakening, followers of the Directory are to direct their minds completely to God by some holy thought such as the following:

Sleep is the image of death and awakening that of the resurrection.

or they may think of that voice that will ring out on the last day:

O dead, arise and come to judgment.

Or they may say with Job:

I know that my Redeemer lives, and that on the last day I will rise again. My God, grant that this be to eternal glory; this hope rests in my inmost being. (Job 19:25-26)

At other times they may say:

On that day, O God, you will call me, and I will answer you; you will stretch forth your right arm to the work of your hands; you have counted all my steps. (Job 14:15-16)

They will make these holy aspirations or others which the Holy Spirit may suggest, for they do have the freedom to follow his inspirations.

After the Angelus they will make the morning exercise, adoring Our Lord from the depths of their being and thanking him for all his benefits. In union with the loving offering which the Savior made of himself to his eternal Father on the tree of the cross, they will offer him their heart, its affections and resolutions, and their whole being, and beg for his help and blessing. They will greet our Lady and ask for her blessing, as well as that of their guardian angel and holy patrons. If they wish, they may say the Our Father. All this should be done quickly and briefly.

As they begin to dress, they will make the Sign of the Cross and say:

Cover me, Lord, with the cloak of innocence and the robe of love. My God, do not let me appear before you stripped of good works.

Direction of Intention

They who wish to thrive and advance in the way of Our Lord should, at the beginning of their actions, both exterior and interior, ask for his grace and offer to his divine Goodness all the good they will do. In this way they will be prepared to bear with peace and serenity all the pain and suffering they will encounter as coming from the fatherly hand of our good God and Savior. His most holy intention is to have them merit by such means in order to reward them afterwards out of the abundance of his love.

They should not neglect this practice in matters which are small and seemingly insignificant, nor even if they are engaged in those things which are agreeable and in complete conformity with their own will and needs, such as drinking, eating, resting, recreating and similar actions. By following the advice of the Apostle, everything they do will be done in God's name to please him alone.

Article 2

Meditation

For meditation they will form themselves by following the instructions in the *Introduction to a Devout Life*, the *Treatise on the Love of God*, the *Spiritual Conferences*, and other good books in harmony with these. They will particularly heed the inspiration of the Holy Spirit and the direction given them. They should never lose time on subtleties nor on supereminent, but unproductive, abstractions. These are nothing more than delusions and deceptions.

The serious practice of this exercise is one of the most important in the religious life.

Preparation of the Day

To form themselves for meditation they will prefer to all other means the exercise of the preparation of the day. Since the preparation makes provision for all their actions, they will make use of it according to varying circumstances. By this means they will endeavor to be disposed to carry out their activities competently and commendably.

Invocation

They will invoke the help of God, saying:

> *Lord, if you do not care for my soul, it is useless that another should do so. (Ps. 127:1)*

They will ask him to make them worthy to spend the day with him without offending him. For this purpose, the words of the psalm may be helpful:

> *Teach me to do your will, for you are my God. Your good spirit will guide me by the hand on level ground. (Ps. 143:10)*

And

> *Your divine majesty by its inexpressible love and boundless charity will give me true life.*

Foresight

This is simply a preview or conjecture of all that could happen during the course of the day. Thus, with the grace of Our Lord, they will wisely and prudently anticipate occasions which could take them by surprise.

Plan of Action

They will carefully plan and seek out the best means to avoid any faults. They will also arrange in an orderly fashion what, in their opinion, is proper for them to do.

Resolution

They will make a firm resolution to obey the will of God, especially during the present day. To this end, they will use the words of the royal prophet David:

> *My soul, will you not cheerfully obey the holy will of God, seeing that your salvation comes from him? (Ps. 62:2)*

Surely this God of infinite majesty and admittedly worthy of every honor and service can only be neglected by us through a lack of courage. Let us, therefore, be consoled and strengthened by this beautiful verse of the psalmist:

> *Let evil men do their worst against me. The Lord, the king, can overcome them all. Let the world complain about me to its heart's content. This means little to me because he who holds sway over all the angelic spirits is my protector. (Ps. 99:1)*

Recommendation

They will entrust themselves and all their concerns into the hands of God's eternal goodness and ask him to consider them as always so commended. Leaving to him the complete care of what they are and what he wants them to be, they will say with all their heart:

> *I have asked you one thing, O Jesus, my Lord, and I shall ask you again and again, namely, that I may faithfully carry out your loving will all the days of my poor and pitiable life. (Ps. 27:4; 40:9)*

> *I commend to you. O gracious Lord, my soul, my life, my heart, my memory, my understanding and my will. Grant that in and with all these, I may serve you, love you, please and honor you forever. (Ps. 31:6; Luke 23:46)*

Article 3

Liturgy of the Hours

It is especially recommended that they show simplicity and readiness in praying the Liturgy of the Hours. Each time they begin, they should place themselves in the presence of God and, in imitation of St. Bernard, ask themselves what they are about to do.

They can also use this method in all their other exercises, so that they may bring to each one the spirit proper to it. They should not have the same deportment and expression at the Liturgy of the Hours as at recreation. In exercises which directly concern the honor and service of God, their spirit should be humble, serious, devout and genuinely loving.

Before beginning the Liturgy of the Hours, they will stir up in themselves similar affections. Then, after the act of adoration, they will offer this action to our Lady and Mother and for the salvation of all creation.

When they say: *O God, come to my assistance*, they should think that Our Lord answers: *Be attentive to my love*.

In order to maintain the proper respect and attention, they should consider from time to time what an honor and privilege it is for them to perform here on earth the same role the angels and saints fulfill in heaven, and that they are praising the same Lord whose majesty makes the highest seraphim tremble.

Article 4

The Mass

First of all they should place themselves in the presence of God. When the celebrant invites the faithful to repentance they should acknowledge their sins, be truly sorry for them and ask God's pardon.

At the Gospel, they will rise promptly to give witness to the fact that they are ready to walk in the way of its precepts saying interiorly:

Jesus Christ was made obedient to death, even to death on the cross. (Phil. 2:8)

As they make the Sign of the Cross, they will declare:

May God be in my mind, on my lips and in my heart, that I may accept his holy Gospel.

If the Profession of Faith is to be said, they should recite it affirming interiorly their willingness to live and die in the belief of the Church.

After the Sanctus they should very humbly and reverently reflect on the blessings conferred by the passion and death of our Savior. They ought to implore him to will their application to the salvation of the whole world, especially to their own and that of all the members of the Church, for the glory and happiness of all the saints and for the relief of the souls in purgatory.

At the elevation of the Blessed Sacrament they are to adore it with deep contrition of heart. Then they will offer it with the celebrant to God the Father for the remission of their own sins and those of the whole world, and offer themselves with the priest and the entire Church. After the elevation they will thank Jesus Christ for his passion and for the institution of this Holy Sacrifice of the Altar.

When the celebrant says the Our Father, they will say it with him with great humility and devotion just as if they were hearing him saying it to the Father and they were repeating it word for word with him.

If someone does not wish to receive Communion sacramentally, he ought to do so spiritually, drawing close to Our Lord by a holy desire to be united with him and to receive him into his heart.

At the blessing they should recall that Jesus Christ is giving them his blessing at the same time.

Article 5

Examination of Conscience

They should examine their conscience twice daily, in the evening and at midday.

In the evening, they will thank Our Lord for all his benefits, especially for his passion, his divine sacrament, the grace of their vocation and for having willed to preserve them during the day, providing for all their needs through this sweet goodness.

They must confess and acknowledge before God that the day has not passed without their having offended him in some way. Because everyone is blind in his own concerns, they should ask for the grace and the light of the Holy Spirit to know their faults clearly.

Then they will begin by reviewing their actions, words and thoughts since their last examination of conscience. Reciting some penitential formula, they will humbly ask Our Lord pardon for their faults.

They will make a firm resolution to correct themselves with the help of God's grace, which they should request with all the love and devotion within their power.

After this, they will recommend their soul, their body, their whole being to the mercy of God. They will pray for the Church, their parents and relatives, and all those toward whom they have a special obligation; they ought not forget the poor souls in purgatory. They should greet our Lady, their guardian angel and holy patrons.

If in their examination they find no faults, let them humble themselves profoundly before God and thank him, admitting nevertheless that they have committed some faults about which they have neither recollection nor awareness.

To make this examination easier, it will be helpful for them when they commit some fault during the day to examine themselves right away, consider briefly their motive, humble themselves before God and make a mental note of this fault in order to include it in the examination that evening.

At the midday examination such formality is not necessary. They need only consider briefly how they have conducted themselves during the morning. If any fault is found, they should add it to the preceding ones and make an act of contrition with a firm purpose of amendment.

To help their memory have a correct knowledge of their faults, they should consider how they have conducted themselves at meditation, at the Liturgy of the Hours, during silence and at community gatherings. If they were engaged in some special work, they will reflect upon what matters were discussed, for here there is danger of failing.

In addition to this examination common to all, they may make a particular one. This concerns the practice of a special virtue most useful to them and directly opposed to those imperfections toward which they feel themselves more inclined.

Article 6

Meals

They should not go to the refectory merely to eat, but to obey God and to take part in a community exercise.

If some tend to be too particular or too eager in eating, they should, upon entering the refectory, make a firm resolution and invoke the grace and help of Our Lord to courageously exercise self-control.

Let him who is too particular consider the gall offered to Our Lord at the height of his bitterest sufferings. Let him who is too eager think of the abstinence and strict fasts of the Fathers of the desert and of so many other saints who so effectively mortified their appetite.

They should never leave the table without having denied themselves in some way. Nevertheless, they ought to eat without hesitation or objection any foods given them for their well-being. With a spirit of indifference they are to accept from the hand of the Lord what they like as well as what they do not like, be it food or anything else.

Recreation

When they recreate, they will ask Our Lord for the grace to say and do only what contributes to his glory. Let them not come to recreation with a sad and disagreeable countenance, but rather with a pleasant and affable one. Just as they should recreate in a spirit of simplicity and openness, so, too, should they take pleasure in speaking often of good and holy topics.

If anyone is inclined to speak too much about himself or is subject to other faults like this, let him, in beginning recreation, briefly recall this imperfection and resolve to be on guard against it. To this end, he should implore the grace of the Holy Spirit and the help of his guardian angel.

They ought not think that there is little virtue in recreating properly. They should not come, therefore, out of habit, or as a matter of form, but with preparation and devotion.

Article 7

Silence

When they begin work, they should say interiorly:

Speak, Lord, your servant is listening [1 Samuel 3:9-10]. O my God, make me worthy to accomplish your holy will.

On entering the appropriate place to do their assigned tasks, they should, in a more special way, put themselves in the presence of God, asking for his grace to make use of silence in accordance with the holy purpose for which it was instituted. This purpose is not only the prevention of idle chatter, but also the curtailing of wandering and useless thoughts while speaking with God, and the obtaining of new strength to work unceasingly in his divine service.

They may make use of their meditation, looking at Our Lord in the mystery which they considered and dwelling on certain points which they particularly appreciated. If, for example, they had meditated on the mystery of the scourging and if the gentle and loving glance which our blessed Savior cast from time to time upon those who were flogging him touched their heart, they should often recall this and then offer the following plea:

O Sweet Jesus, look down on me with your merciful eyes, or, Lord, take away from me anything that might be displeasing in your sight.

They may remain quietly at the feet of Our Lord, listen to what he will say to their heart, consider his goodness and love, and speak to him from time to time with heartfelt aspirations, and with these or similar ejaculatory prayers:

To Almighty God: O God, you are my Father. My God, have mercy on my weakness. O Lord, let me live only for you.

To the Blessed Virgin: Mother of mercy, pray for me.

To their guardian angel: O glorious angel, my protector, pray for me.

In like manner they should address the saints toward whom they have a special devotion.

At each hour, let them regret hours wasted and recall that they will have to give an account of this hour and of all the moments of their life. Let them remember that they are approaching eternity, that hours are centuries to the damned, that they are running toward death, and that perhaps their last hour may soon be at hand.

After such thoughts, they should make devout aspirations that God be merciful to them at that last hour. This certainly will happen for those who have been very faithful in doing this. They ought to practice this at all times and on all occasions. By this means they will grow and progress daily from virtue to virtue, even to the perfection of divine love.

Those who suffer from some strong temptation or emotion can find courage and strength in considering the pains of Our Lord, picturing him undergoing them.

When they experience difficulty in the practice of virtues, they will be enlightened and aided if they consider him in the exercise of those virtues which he practiced while on earth.

Article 8

Retiring

While undressing, they should keep their mind attentive as much as possible to the point to be taken for meditation.

In bed they ought to remember that Our Lord and some saints used to sleep on the cold ground, and how much they are obliged to love and serve him, since his gentle goodness provides for their slightest comforts in such a fatherly way. Lying there, they should picture to themselves that one day they will be like this in the grave and ask God to assist them at the hour of death. Let them act as if they were seeing Our Lord with their own eyes, for he really sees them in this action as well as in any other.

They should always try to fall asleep with some good thought.

Thoughts of St. Francis de Sales for the Night:

If they awaken during the night, they will stir up their heart immediately with these words:

> At midnight someone shouted: The groom is here! Come out and greet him. (Matt. 25:6)

From the view of the darkness around them, they will turn to a consideration of the darkness of their own soul and of all sinners and offer this prayer:

> O Lord, since your merciful heart made you come down from heaven to earth to visit us, please enlighten those who lie prostrate in the darkness of ignorance and in the shadow of eternal death; if it be your will, guide them also into the path of interior peace. (Luke 1:78-79)

At times they will turn to their God, their Savior, and say:

You neither slumber nor sleep, you who guard the Israel of our souls (Ps. 121:7). The most intense darkness of midnight can present no obstacle to your divine activity; at that hour you were born of the holy virgin, your Mother; at that hour, too, you can cause your heavenly graces to be born in our souls and completely fill us with your choicest blessings. Merciful Redeemer, so enlighten my poor blind heart with the beautiful rays of your grace that it may never remain in any way in the death of sin; O, I beg you, do not allow my invisible enemies to say: We have overcome him (Ps. 13:4).

Finally, after having considered the darkness and the imperfections of their soul, they may say with Isaiah:

Watchman, watchman, does much of the night of our imperfections still remain? (Isa. 21:11-12)

And they will hear him answer them:

The morning of good inspirations has come; why do you love the darkness more than the light? (John 3:19)

In addition, they may use these holy words:

Neither the sun nor its rays are my principal light, but God alone, who is as merciful to me by night as he is by day.

Article 9

Confession

When they wish to go to confession they will prepare themselves in this manner.

In a spirit of deep humility at the feet of their crucified Lord, they will ask for the grace and light of the Holy Spirit to discern their faults well. Then they should recall everything they have found in their daily examinations since their previous confession and consider for a moment if there is anything else. After this, let them humbly ask Our Lord for pardon and for the grace to correct themselves. For this purpose they will make a firm resolution, especially concerning the more important things they have noticed. They will renounce their faults and attempt to stir up true sorrow for them, however slight they may be, because it is always too great an evil to have been displeasing to the sovereign goodness of our Savior who is so merciful to us each day.

After having noticed their current faults, they should add something from the past which is clearly sinful and make an act of contrition for all these together. Then they will go humbly to their confessor honoring God and the sacred priesthood in the person of the priest. They ought to look upon him in confession as an angel whom God sends to reconcile them to his divine goodness.

Let them be brief and clear in their confession. Let them never confess out of routine or scrupulosity, but rather out of devotion and attention as in an action of great importance and value.

Article 10

Holy Communion

The principal intention which they should have at Holy Communion is union with Our Lord.

To prepare themselves better for this union, it would be good, in their prayer and recollection the evening before, to raise their thoughts somewhat to Our Lord in this sacrament. They should stir up in their soul a holy reverence and spiritual joy that they should be so blessed as to receive our gentle Savior. Then they ought to renew their decision to serve him fervently. When they have received him, they can reaffirm this decision, not by a vow, but by a good and holy resolution.

At the moment of communion, they could use some mental or vocal aspirations, such as that of St. Francis:

Who am I, Lord, and who are you?

or perhaps that of St. Elizabeth:

Where does this blessing come from — that my Lord should come to me? (Luke 1:43) or that of St. John the Evangelist:

Yes, come, Lord Jesus. (Rev. 22:20)

After Holy Communion they should consider Our Lord seated in their heart as on his throne and bring before him, one after the other, their faculties and senses to hear his commands and promise him fidelity. They can also summon their soul to some holy affections such as:

Fear of displeasing and losing the Lord—They will say with David:

My Lord, be not far from me. (Ps. 38:22)

or with the travelers on the road to Emmaus:

Stay with us. It is nearly evening. (Luke 24:29)

Confidence and courage—again with David:

I will fear no evil because you are at my side, Lord. (Ps. 23:4)

Love—with the Spouse they will say:

My lover belongs to me and I to him; he will rest in my heart; I have found him whom my heart loves. I will not let him go. (Song of Songs 2:16; 1:13; 3:4)

Thanksgiving:

O Lord, because you have given me this great grace, I will bless you eternally and forever, and I will make your praises as countless as the stars of the sky. (Gen. 22:16-19)

Determination to serve the Lord—with the words of Jacob:

The Lord shall be my God, and the stone of my heart, heretofore hardened, will be his abode. (Gen. 28:21-22)

They can also think of the interior fervor of our Lady, her devotion, her humility, her confidence and her courage when the angel told her that the Holy Spirit would come into her. They can recall, too, that at the same time that she understood that God was giving her his heart, namely, his Son, she in turn gave herself to God and her soul was overwhelmed with love. They, too, receive a similar grace in Communion. It is not an angel, but Jesus Christ himself who assures them that in this action the Holy Spirit comes into them and in a way Christ is conceived and born in them. O God, what delight and peace!

Consequently after this consideration the soul can truly say as did this holy Lady:

> I am the servant of the Lord. Let it be done to me according to his word which he spoke from his sacred mouth, that whoever feeds on him remains in him and he in them, and that whoever feeds on him will live for him, by him and in him and will live forever (Luke 1:38; John 6:50, 55-59).

For both Holy Mass and Holy Communion, they may use these thoughts or such others as the Holy Spirit will suggest to them.

Each month they will offer Holy Communion for:

- the renewal of their vows

- the Church, the Pope and the clergy

- the preservation of the Congregation and the maintenance therein of union and mutual charity

- the conversion of sinners and of those who do not belong to the faith

- all the needs of the people

Advice of St. Francis de Sales
on the Directory

It is true that the Directory proposes many exercises. Yet it is good and fitting to keep one's interior orderly and busy in the beginning. When, however, after a period of time, persons have put into practice somewhat this multiplicity of interior actions, have become formed and habituated to them and spiritually agile in their use, then the practices should coalesce into a single exercise of greater simplicity: either into a love of complacency, or a love of benevolence, or a love of confidence, or of union and reunion of the heart to the will of God. This multiplicity thus becomes unity.

Moreover, if there be someone, even in the novitiate, who fears too much this submission to the exercises indicated, provided this fear does not come from whim, presumption, contempt or annoyance, a prudent director may lead him by another way, even though ordinarily, as experience has shown, the practices of the Directory are useful.

Appendix 2

HELPFUL RESOURCES FOR LIVING WELL

ONLINE RESOURCES

The electronic library of the Salesian Center for Faith and Culture at DeSales University offers links to numerous books, monographs, articles, and reflections on Salesian spirituality. http://web1.desales.edu/default.aspx?pageid=10521

The website of DeSales Resources and Ministries offers an online catalogue of works in Salesian spirituality, including editions of out-of-print books, and provides access to the special collection of Salesian studies housed at DeSales University. http://embracedbygod.org/product-category/books-recordings/

Fr. Joseph Boenzi, S.D.B., has compiled a bibliography of English-language works in Salesian spirituality that is available online through the Salesian Center for Faith and Culture. http://web1.desales.edu/assets/salesian/PDF/Boenzibib-lio1996.pdf

BIOGRAPHIES

Boenzi, Joseph. *Saint Francis de Sales: Life and Spirit*. Stella Niagra, NY: DeSales Resource Center, 2013.

Camus, Jean Pierre. *The Spirit of St. Francis de Sales, Bishop and Prince of Geneva*. London: Longmans, Green, and Co., 1921.

Dailey, Thomas F. "The 'Real' Story on St. Francis de Sales!" *Theological Review of the Episcopal Academy*, December 2005, http://web1.desales.edu/assets/salesian/PDF/DaileyRealStory.pdf.

Ravier, Andre. *Francis de Sales: Sage and Saint*. Translated by Joseph Bowler, O.S.F.S. San Francisco: Ignatius Press, 1988.

Stopp, Elisabeth. *St. Francis de Sales: A Testimony by St. Chantal*. Hyattsville, MD: Institute of Salesian Studies, 1967.

Wright, Wendy M. *Bond of Perfection: Jeanne de Chantal and François de Sales*. Mahwah, NJ: Paulist Press, 1986.

PRIMARY SOURCES
(WRITTEN BY ST. FRANCIS DE SALES)

Introduction to the Devout Life

Introduction to the Devout Life. Translated and edited by John K. Ryan. New York: Image Books, 1972/2003.

Introduction to the Devout Life. Christian Classics Ethereal Library, 2002, http://www.ccel.org/ccel/desales/devout_life.

Introduction to the Devout Life. Charlotte, NC: TAN Books, 2010.

Letters of St. Francis de Sales

Francis de Sales, Jane de Chantal: Letters of Spiritual Direction. Translated by Péronne Marie Thibert, V.H.M. Selected and introduced by Wendy M. Wright and Joseph F. Power, O.S.F.S. New York/Mahwah, NJ: Paulist Press, 1988.

Letters to Persons in Religion. Volume 4 of the Library of St. Francis de Sales. Translated by Henry B. Mackey. London: Burns and Oates, 1909.

Letters to Persons in the World. Volume 1 of the Library of St. Francis de Sales. Translated by Henry B. Mackey. New York: Benzinger Brothers, 1890.

Roses Among Thorns: Simple Advice for Renewing Your Spiritual Journey. Edited and translated by Christopher O. Blum. Manchester, NH: Sophia Institute Press, 2014.

Serenity of Heart: Bearing the Troubles of This Life. Manchester, NH: Sophia Institute Press, 1997.

St. Francis de Sales: Selected Letters. Translated by Elisabeth Stopp. New York: Harper and Row, 1960.

Thy Will Be Done: Letters to Persons in the World. Manchester, NH: Sophia Institute Press, 1995.

Sermons

Sermons of St. Francis de Sales series. Translated by the Nuns of the Visitation. Edited by Lewis Fiorelli, O.S.F.S. TAN Books.

> For Advent and Christmas (1987)
>
> For Lent, Given in 1622 (1987)
>
> On Our Lady (1985)
>
> On Prayer (1985)

Sermons on the Eucharist. Translated by Alexander T. Pocetto, O.S.F.S. Introduction by Thomas F. Dailey, O.S.F.S. Commentary by James F. Cryan, O.S.F.S. Center Valley, PA: Salesian Center for Faith and Culture, 2005.

Sermon Texts on Saint Joseph. Translated by Joseph F. Chorpenning. Toronto: Peregrina, 2000.

The Spiritual Conferences

The Art of Loving God: Simple Virtues for the Christian Life. Manchester, NH: Sophia Institute Press, 1998.

The Spiritual Conferences. Translated under the supervision of Francis A. Gasquet and Henry B. Mackey. London: Burns and Oates, 1909.

The Spiritual Conferences of St. Francis de Sales. Translated by William Ruhl. Washington, DC: DeSales Spirituality Center, 1997.

The Spiritual Exercises

Spiritual Exercises. Translated by William N. Dougherty, O.S.F.S. Edited with an introductory essay, notes, and bio-bibliographical note by Joseph Chorpenning, O.S.F.S. Toronto: Peregrina, 1993.

Treatise on the Love of God

Finding God's Will for You. Manchester, NH: Sophia Institute Press, 1998.

Treatise on the Love of God. Translated by Dom Henry Benedict Mackey. Rockford, IL: TAN Books, 1997.

Treatise on the Love of God. Christian Classics Ethereal Library, http://www.ccel.org/ccel/desales/love.html.

Treatise on the Love of God. 2 vols. Translated with an introduction and notes by John K. Ryan. Rockford, IL: Tan Books, 1975.

Other Works by St. Francis de Sales

"Advice to Confessors." Translated by Joseph M. Baraniewicz, O.S.F.S. Hyattsville, MD: Institute of Salesian Studies, 1969.

The Catholic Controversy: A Defense of the Faith. Translated by Henry B. Mackey. Rockford, IL: TAN Books, 2009.

Consoling Thoughts series. Compiled by Père Huget. TAN Books, 2013:

> On Eternity
>
> On God and Providence
>
> On Sickness and Death
>
> On Trials of an Interior Life

"A Little Treatise on Holy Communion." Written for Madame Rose Bourgeois, Abbess of Puits-d'Orbe. Translated by Alexander Pocetto, O.S.F.S. Center Valley, PA: Salesian Center for Faith and Culture, 2005.

On the Preacher and Preaching. Translated by John K. Ryan. Chicago: Henry Regnery, 1964.

The Sign of the Cross: The Fifteen Most Powerful Words in the English Language. Edited and translated by Christopher O. Blum. Manchester, NH: Sophia Institute Press, 2013.

SECONDARY SOURCES

On The Spiritual Directory

Dailey, Thomas. "Jewel of Perfection: The *Spiritual Directory* as a Privileged Means of Propagating the Salesian Spirit," *Indian Journal of Spirituality* 21/4 (2008): 349-362.

Fiorelli, Lewis. *Spiritual Directory of St. Francis de Sales: Reflections for the Laity.* Boston: Pauline Books, 1985.

Pocetto, Alexander. "The *Spiritual Directory* in the American Oblate Tradition," Center Valley, PA: Salesian Center for Faith and Culture, 2008.

On Salesian Spirituality

Dailey, Thomas. *Praying with Francis de Sales*. Winona, MN: Saint Mary's Press, 1997/Frederick, MD: Word Among Us Press, 1998.

Power, Joseph. *Francis de Sales: Finding God Wherever You Are*. New Rochelle, NY: New City Press, 1993.

Stopp, Elisabeth. *A Man to Heal Differences: Essays and Talks on St. Francis de Sales*. Philadelphia: St. Joseph's University Press, 1997.

Wright, Wendy M. *Francis de Sales: Essential Writings*. New York: Crossroad, 1994.

Wright, Wendy M. *Heart Speaks to Heart: The Salesian Tradition* [Traditions of Christian Spirituality]. Maryknoll, NY: Orbis Books, 2004.

Wright, Wendy M. *A Retreat with Francis de Sales, Jane de Chantal and Aelred of Rievaulx: Befriending Each Other in God*. Cincinnati: Saint Anthony Messenger Press, 1996.

REVEREND THOMAS F. DAILEY, O.S.F.S.

Reverend Thomas F. Dailey, O.S.F.S., is the Blessed Louis Brisson Chair in Salesian Spirituality and Professor of Theology at DeSales University in Center Valley, Pennsylvania. There he founded and still directs the Salesian Center for Faith and Culture. He is also the author of *Praying with Francis de Sales* (St. Mary's Press, 1997) and has published articles about Salesian spirituality in *Homiletic and Pastoral Review*, the *Journal of Catholic Higher Education*, *Review for Religious*, and *Studia Mystica*. He frequently offers conferences and retreats based on the Salesian tradition.

An Invitation

Reader, the book that you hold in your hands was published by Sophia Institute Press. Sophia Institute seeks to nurture the spiritual, moral, and cultural life of souls and to spread the Gospel of Christ in conformity with the authentic teachings of the Roman Catholic Church.

Our press fulfills this mission by offering translations, reprints, and new publications that afford readers a rich source of the enduring wisdom of mankind.

We also operate two popular online Catholic resources: CrisisMagazine.com and CatholicExchange.com.

Crisis Magazine provides insightful cultural analysis that arms readers with the arguments necessary for navigating the ideological and theological minefields of the day. *Catholic Exchange* provides world news from a Catholic perspective as well as daily devotionals and articles that will help you to grow in holiness and live a life consistent with the teachings of the Church.

In 2013, Sophia Institute launched Sophia Institute for Teachers to renew and rebuild Catholic culture through service to Catholic education. With the goal of nurturing the spiritual, moral, and cultural life of souls, and an abiding respect for the role and work of teachers, we strive to provide materials and programs that are at once enlightening to the mind and ennobling to the heart; faithful and complete, as well as useful and practical.

www.SophiaInstitute.com
www.CatholicExchange.com
www.CrisisMagazine.com
www.SophiaInstituteforTeachers.org

Sophia Institute Press® is a registered trademark of Sophia Institute. Sophia Institute is a tax-exempt institution as defined by the Internal Revenue Code, Section 501(c)(3). Tax I.D. 22-2548708.